Portable feasts

Portable feasts

Clare Ferguson

Photography by **Jeremy Hopley**

LAUREL GLEN

Dedication

To my parents, whose pleasure in decent food, good cooking, conviviality, and picnicking set me up for life, and to my sisters, Alison and Patricia, who, like me, continue these traditions, with love and laughter, to this very day.

I also thank my husband, Ian, for his love and encouragement.

Notes:
- *All measures are level unless otherwise stated.*
- *Fresh herbs should be used unless otherwise stated. If substituting dried herbs use a half or a quarter the amount. Better still, substitute another fresh herb.*
- *Dishes that contain uncooked or partly cooked eggs, raw milk cheeses, or rare-cooked meats should not be consumed by infants, young children, pregnant and nursing mothers, the elderly or anyone with a weakened immune system.*

Published in 2001 by
Laurel Glen Publishing
An imprint of the Advantage Publishers Group
5880 Oberlin Drive, San Diego, CA 92121-4794
www.advantagebooksonline.com

Text copyright © Clare Ferguson 2001
Photography, design and layout copyright © Jacqui Small 2001

Library of Congress Cataloging-in-Publication Data.

Ferguson, Clare.

   Portable Feasts/Clare Ferguson; photography by Jeremy Hopley.
   p.cm.

   ISBN 1–57145–515–9
   1. Outdoor cookery. 1. Title

TX823. F43 2001
641.5'78–dc21

00-067757

Publisher Jacqui Small

Editor Madeline Weston

Designer Robin Rout

Additional photography Robin Rout

Food stylist Clare Ferguson

Assistant food stylist Bethany Heald

Stylist Wei Tang

Production Geoff Barlow

North American Edition

Publisher Allen Orso

Managing Editor JoAnn Padgett

Product Development Editor Elizabeth McNulty

Project Editor Bobby Wong

Assisting Editor Mana Monzavi

Printed and bound in China.

Contents

Some of my fondest childhood memories involve food eaten outdoors or in unorthodox situations. As a busy adult, such activities still delight me. After a long day's work or a complicated week, I am often to be found coaxing my husband, neighbors, and friends into joining me for an open-air feast in the local park.

Friends may be urged to provide some chilled wine, beers, or mineral water. We two will pillage the fridge and the pantry: grab olives, olive oil, pepper and salt grinders, lemons, cold fish pâté, and a crisp cucumber or lettuce. Along will come a package of cookies or chocolate bars. Packed into our baskets will be plates, cutlery, glasses, a corkscrew, and paper napkins. In seconds we are off.

En route we will pick up a freshly cooked rotisserie chicken, foil-wrapped, and some crusty rolls or baguettes. If the melons or grapes look and smell good, we'll buy some of these, too.

When we all meet up at the park and select our favorite bench in a niche in the mossy walls, we sit back, survey the flowers, and breathe a long sigh. Some of the stresses and strains of our lives unravel. Corks fly. Bottles pop. Glasses clink. The joy of spending precious time among friends, feasting, is something I find to be both restorative and fascinating.

Portable Feasts celebrates informality and fun; it elevates casual eating to an art.

Choose from over a hundred ideas; a collection of "little feasts," sumptuous appetizers and hors d'oeuvre, with drinks to match. Or select some sandwiches, pastries, and cakes for a late lunch outdoors. Maybe you'd prefer some main dishes served warm straight from their containers or some barbecue bounty cooked right on the spot? On the following pages you will find all these, along with appealing sweet feasts which are also portable: fresh fruit desserts, baking, and fanciful cookies.

Food should be inspirational but easy. With this in mind, many of the ideas are intriguing, multicultural dishes. Included are many fascinating spicy dressings, seasonings, marinades, ethnic wraps, and salads; interesting pâtés, dips, and spreads as well as magnificent main-course dishes. There are kabobs, pasta dishes, and brownies; cocktails, old-fashioned cordials and herbal teas.

Sand in the sandwiches? This is nobody's idea of fun. Advice about how to prepare, pack, and present these delicacies is built in to the book's structure along with countless full-page color photographs. Often taken on site, these pictures enliven each situation. Food must arrive at its destination fresh, safe, and undamaged. Appropriate containers and serving tools are also considered, and much of the pleasure of eating out of doors comes from showing off your feast to advantage. This is a talent you can easily acquire.

Follow the many professional tips we have included in this book and any portable feast you make will be sure to be a success.

Basic common sense helps make meals on the move more enjoyable and less fraught with mishaps. Butter is no use if it is a liquid pool on the bottom of the container; strawberry jam tastes best from an unbroken container, wine is frustrating when you've forgotten your corkscrew or the glasses.

It is easy to develop an instinct for organization and a spirit for innovation. *Portable Feasts* celebrates both of these concepts along with a belief in delicious, fresh food, attractively served. But where? The venue can be anywhere you choose. The location is up to you.

A leisurely trip to the ball game or to a school sports day will be more memorable if you've managed to take a few delicious snacks and drinks for having en route.

Portable Feasts provides ideas for meals, snacks, and drinks for those on the move: romantic suppers for couples; children's picnics under the trees, fun for everyone. The recipes were developed to complement one another, resulting in scores of menu combinations to suit many different occasions.

When planning your meal consider pairing up recipes that can be prepared in advance with others that can be done on the spot: sautéed, grilled, or bonfire-cooked dishes. Combine with these some good quality delicatessen food, fresh produce, breads, cheeses, beers, wines, and fruit juices. Not only does this make the planning simpler but it also makes each meal a unique event. Local specialties—such as fresh seafood, fresh herbs, orchard fruits growing on the trees—can be additions which become celebrations in their own right.

Finally, participation on the part of your fellow eaters, can make this mode of entertaining much more democratic and far more fun. Children may surprise you; those who would not dream of peeling the potatoes at home may prove expert at wraps and kabobs. Partners who profess to be novices in the kitchen often blossom into people precise at packing picnic hampers, brilliant at building a barbecue, and gifted at making a gin fizz.

For them, and for you, this book is a celebration of the possible; and how you can make epicures of everyone. Enjoy your own portable feasts, wherever they may be.

Picnic essentials

Keeping food or drink perfectly fresh, and at the right temperature, requires some ingenuity, but not necessarily expense. Household items such as coolers, vacuum flasks, take-out containers, screw-top jars and bottles, and snap-top plastic containers can all be used. Plastic buckets, bowls, or bags; bottle carriers as well as wooden hampers, wickerwork, or metal boxes, can all be pressed into service. Metal cutlery, chopsticks, shatterproof glasses, and durable crockery will often fit the bill.

But there is also, now, a superb selection of specially designed picnic sets made from colorful, unbreakable plastic, melamine, metal, woven fibers, and shatterproof glass. There are also disposables: paper plates, cups, napkins, and plastic cutlery.

On-site cooking needs special equipment: camping gas cookers, portable cooking rings, and wind-proof stoves are possibilities. Go to camping and leisure stores. Many barbecues exist: some tiny, disposable and inexpensive, others robust, large gas-fired charbroilers.

Outdoor fires and pit cooking are fun for the more adventurous—but do so safely—and take kindling, aromatic woods, charcoal, and scented herbs for added savor. Don't forget the corkscrew and the cushions!

A folding plastic carrying box is ideal for holding all your food containers as well as plastic cups and vacuum flasks.

A strongly woven nylon bag with handles to carry your picnic. The plastic boxes all have snap-top lids to keep food fresh.

A neatly divided lunch box keeps different foods separate; stacking plastic tumblers is both safe and space saving.

The old-fashioned ginger ale bottle keeps drinks, carbonated and still, secure; carry your bottles in an ice bucket.

Your ice bucket can be converted into a bowl for washing dishes when the feasting is over. Take a brush along with you.

Stainless steel cutlery may be heavier but it is a pleasure to use. Bowls and buckets are useful for salads and ice.

This camping stove, using denatured alcohol for fuel, cleverly packs away to make it easy to carry. See right.

Unpacked, the stove contains a kettle, three pans, and a skillet. Lightweight, it is useful for cooking for small numbers.

A windproof stove, burning camping gas, and a lightweight kettle mean you can have a hot drink literally anywhere!

Vacuum flasks come in many sizes and styles: stainless steel, plastic, and shatterproof glass or ceramic are all practical.

This small portable barbecue is made of galvanized metal and has its own grill rack. It has a drawer to remove the ash.

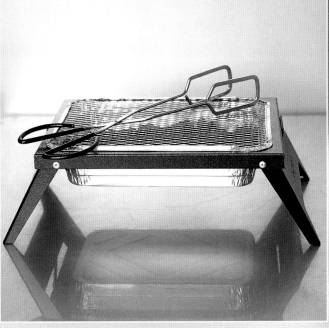

This ingenious grill has a disposable tray which is set into a folding metal holder, providing easy clean up.

This cast-iron grill can be placed directly over charcoal started in a fire pit or other fire-safe place.

This large galvanized metal grill can be found in Greek shops. The rack folds back to cook kabobs over the coals.

Useful items include a jackknife, can opener, tongs, oyster knife, corkscrew, camping plates, and wooden spoons.

Galvanized metal storage boxes with handles could carry camping storage containers and stainless mixing bowls.

Wooden carrying hampers are stylish and practical with sliding lids and rope handles. Wrap your dishes in napkins.

Durable melamine picnic dishes and attractive wooden cutlery are easily transported in a tough plastic shopping bag.

A wire basket makes the ideal carrier for shatterproof glasses, each wrapped in a pretty table napkin.

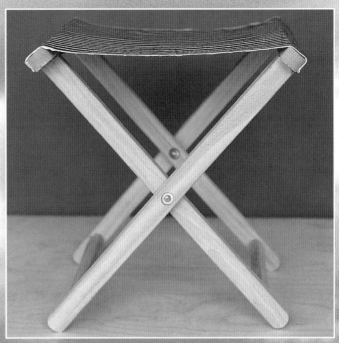

A stool or a table, according to your needs. This lightweight camping stool can double up as either and is easy to carry.

Rugs, throws, and cushions are an essential. Sit on them, eat off them, and lie back and rest after the picnic is over.

Picnicking at dusk? A gas lamp and lanters will light your feast. Citronella candles will keep mosquitoes at bay.

Small feasts

Delicious snacks and appetizers can do more than awaken the appetite, they can enliven the whole meal. Sometimes one item alone is enough for a splendid little feast. Follow it with a crisp or juicy piece of fresh fruit, add a glass of sparkling water, some juice, wine, or beer and suddenly you've made a perfectly balanced small feast.

Alternatively combine several snack items from this chapter for an *al fresco* party or use one recipe in the time-honored way, as the first of several courses. Many choices are included here; enjoy yourself selecting and combining them to suit your own particular occasion.

Radishes, French Style *page 18*

Tapenade *page 20*

Green Pea & Prosciutto Soup *page 32*

The recipes in this first chapter are appetite-arousing, delicious snacks and small savory items. These can be eaten on their own, grouped together informally as a snack meal, or teamed up with other dishes from the following chapters to make more complex menus.

When combining recipes do not be too ambitious. Two or three new ideas at the most, combined with some ready-made, store-bought items such as bread, cheese, fruit, and something good to drink, would seem a realistic aim.

On the other hand, combining a beautiful bunch of fresh radishes with butter and salt may be an entirely novel concept. It is utterly delectable. Clean, fresh, crisp, and still-cold radishes in a leafy bunch; some perfect butter, flaky salt: such choices not only make sense but add pleasure and give style to the most minimal of meals.

Do not underestimate the importance of contrast: sophisticated foods with earthy ones; hot with cold; rich with plain; spicy with mild; let colors remain vivid: leave good-looking produce whole whenever possible, not only because it looks more lovely, but because it is likely to retain more of its original food value as well. And it saves time and effort.

Be creative: smoked trout pâté and matzo crackers may work wonderfully with borscht or black bean soup, served in bowls you can sip from. Salted almonds followed by fritters with a flask of hot pea soup may be just the thing on a cool day in spring. "Palm leaves" (palmiers), spiced cheese and green

salad may seem enough for a minifeast. Blini and taramasalata, without the salmon "caviar" (salmon caviar being sophisticated fare) may be best eaten alone.

Suit your drinks to your circumstances: drivers must be offered nonalcoholic alternatives. Anyway there are wonderful soft drinks, and herb- and fruit-based drinks you can offer, as well as alcohol-free cocktails of great charm and freshness. The alternative is to buy some still or sparkling spring water en route, some oranges, limes, or a grapefruit, and a bag of ice cubes. This way you make fabulous fresh drinks to order, on the spot. (But be sure to have packed unbreakable glasses or else carry ordinary goblets in a wire tray or wrap up each glass in a cloth napkin).

Tapenade with soft-boiled eggs and baguette: some crisp, salad leaves, followed by new potatoes with blue cheese, makes a picnic fit for a king.

Mini game burgers then some tagliatelle pasta with truffle butter, a bunch or two of black grapes or some dried muscat raisins, teamed with a formidable Côtes du Rhône or a Syrah and you'll feel that autumn's bounty is a celebration in itself.

Imagination, delectable recipe ideas, decent bread, appropriate wine, seasonal fruits and regional produce, and you have every chance of becoming a picnic and portable feast *aficionado.*

So relax, and *bon appétit*—use these ideas to devise your very own, easy style of entertaining. These small appetizers make an excellent start.

Parmesan & Poppy Seed "Palm Leaves" (palmiers)

These pretty pastries are a savory version of the classic sweet ones. Paradoxically, they taste good dusted with powdered sugar. To carry them, pack them into a cloth-lined box or shallow basket.

Makes 32–36

Ingredients

1 lb. 10 oz. store-bought puff pastry, whole or prerolled (defrosted if frozen)

4 tbsp. Dijon mustard

4 tbsp. black poppy seeds

4 tbsp. freshly grated parmesan cheese

2 tbsp. powdered sugar

To prepare/cook Roll out or unfold the chilled pastry into a rectangle about 8 x 28 in., and about 1/8 in. thick. Trim the edges. Spread the pastry first with mustard, then poppy seeds, then cheese. Starting from both short sides, roll each in tightly toward the center so that they meet in a double roll with a "ram's horn" appearance. Turn the double roll over so that the flat side is up. Using a long, serrated knife and pressing firmly, slice across to give 32–36 slim "palm leaves" (palmiers). Spray 4 or more baking sheets with water and lay the "palm leaves" on them, allowing space between each. Chill for 1 hour. Bake 2 sheets at a time in an oven preheated to 450°F for 6–7 minutes or until they start to caramelize underneath. With a small, narrow spatula carefully turn each "palm leaf" over. Bake again for a further 4–5 minutes or until crispy and caramelized. Repeat with the remaining "palm leaves" until they are all cooked. Cool completely on wire racks. Store in an airtight container for up to 7 days.

To present Dust them lightly with powdered sugar, using a fine sieve, at serving time.

Radishes, French Style

The French treat radishes with a respect they are rarely accorded in other countries. The crunch of radish, a dot of butter, a tingle of sea salt flakes—and the meal is under way. Select beautiful radishes: crimson or pink and white, in fat bunches, leaves intact. Choose fresh butter, maybe from your farmers' market, and sea salt flakes.

Serves 4

Ingredients

2–3 bunches fresh, crisp radishes with leaves

unsalted or lightly salted butter

2 oz. sea salt flakes or kosher salt

To prepare Pack the washed, chilled radishes in a cloth-lined basket or box with the (room temperature) butter and a lidded small pot of salt.

To present Encourage your companions to break off a radish, dunk in butter, dip in salt, and eat.

Note:

Some good sourdough bread might be a nice accompaniment.

Spiced Cheese

with Crudités

This is based on a dish popular in Hungary and Austria; a soft, fresh, mild but spreadable cheese, traditionally served surrounded by heaps of salt, paprika, mustard, butter, chives, and caraway seeds. In this version they are all stirred in. Try this spread with crisp, seasonal vegetables cut into sticks; it is hugely adaptable. Chill well before taking out of doors, especially if on active pursuits.

Makes about 1 lb., Serves 8

Ingredients

scant 1 1/2 cups curd cheese, cream cheese, or low-fat soft cheese

1/4 cup salted butter

2 tbsp. hot mustard powder

2 tsp. hot red paprika

2 tbsp. freshly grated horseradish (optional)

2 tbsp. chopped fresh chives

1/2 tsp. salt

2 tbsp. caraway seeds

Crudités:
Choose from cucumber, bell peppers, scallions, onion rings, button mushrooms, cherry tomatoes, carrot, and perhaps breadsticks, crispbreads, and crackers.

To prepare Cream the cheese and butter together until well blended, and stir in all the remaining ingredients. Pack in individual snap-top boxes or bowls. Put the selection of crudités in a second, rigid container, so they stay undamaged in transit.

Salted Almonds

These treats, learned from a Greek cook, are blissfully simple but very appealing. Once made and completely cold, they'll keep for ages in an airtight jar. And although they look dark, they have a satisfying crunch and superb taste. A great snack.

Makes about 1 1/4 lb.

Ingredients

4 cups shelled, unblanched almonds

6 tbsp. freshly squeezed lemon juice

4 tbsp. table salt

To prepare/cook Spread out the almonds in 2 large flat ovenproof trays or dishes, such as roasting tins. Pour the lemon juice over the almonds and leave until well absorbed; about 20 minutes. Drain off excess liquid. Sprinkle the salt over and turn the almonds in it so that they are coated. Bake the almonds, uncovered, in an oven preheated to 350°F, toward the top, for 35–45 minutes, stirring twice. Cool in the tins. Once the nuts are completely cold, scoop them up, shaking off the excess salt, and pack into airtight jars. They keep for weeks. To transport, take handfuls from the jar and pack into a twist of foil or waxed paper, secured with some string.

To present Undo the paper or foil twist and let people help themselves.

Tapenade with Eggs & Baguette

Provençale tapenade is a revelation; the flavors sing out and it looks dark and glossy. It is essential to ensure all your ingredients are superb. This generous tapenade recipe makes enough for 4 meals; it keeps well in the refrigerator for weeks, though its accompaniments must always be fresh on the day.

Makes about 1 1/4 lb. tapenade, Serves 16
Presentation serves 4

Ingredients

3 1/2 cups dry-cured salted black olives

6 1/2 oz. canned tuna in olive oil

3 1/2 oz. canned anchovies, drained, and chopped

3 oz. pickled or salted capers

5–6 garlic cloves, crushed

2 tsp. fresh thyme leaves or 1/2 tsp. dried

2 tbsp. extra-virgin olive oil

1–2 tbsp. cognac or brandy

4 free-range, organic eggs

1 baguette loaf

To prepare Pit the olives. Put the olives, the tuna, flaked, and its oil, the anchovies, and capers (well rinsed in warm water, twice), and the garlic and thyme into a large mortar or food-processor. Pound using a pestle, or process, in brief bursts, in the food-processor, to a rough black paste. Now drizzle in the olive oil, continuing to pound or process, making the paste glossier still. Finally stir in the cognac or brandy. Spoon into a large lidded pot or bowl. Refrigerate. To soft-boil the eggs, allow them to come to room temperature, cover them with very warm water, bring to a boil, and simmer for 4–5 minutes. Cool under running cold water. When ready to pack the picnic, scoop about 2 oz. tapenade per person into a transportable container. Remove the eggshells and pack the eggs separately.

To present When at the site, halve the eggs across. Slice or tear some baguette. Surround the tapenade with egg halves and bread. Encourage diners to dip the egg into the tapenade and eat, alternating egg with a bite of baguette.

Hummus

This Middle Eastern dip and spread, which, strictly, should be called *hummus bi tahini*, since it contains tahini (not all versions of hummus do) is delicious when made at home, even if you use canned chickpeas.

Makes about 1 1/2 lb.

Ingredients

1 1/4 lb. freshly cooked or canned chickpeas (about 8 oz. if cooked from dry)

3 tbsp. toasted sesame seed paste (tahini)

4 tbsp. freshly squeezed lemon juice

4 garlic cloves, crushed

3/4 tsp. salt

1/2 cup extra-virgin olive oil

To serve:

Paprika, flatleaf parsley, optional flatbreads

To prepare/cook Drain the cooked chickpeas but reserve some of the liquid. Put the chickpeas into a food processor with the tahini, juice, garlic, and salt. Process in several long bursts to a gritty paste. With the machine running, drizzle in 7 tbsp. of the olive oil through the feed tube until you have a thick, rich, creamy purée. Do not overprocess. If it seems too dense, or intense, process again, in brief bursts, adding 6–8 tbsp. of cooking liquid, until it is the texture you like. Serve the hummus cool, straight away, or chill it if it is to be used at a later time; it keeps well, in the refrigerator, for up to 1 week.

To present Serve with the reserved olive oil drizzled over the hummus in its bowl, a pinch of paprika and some parsley sprigs, adding warmed torn flatbreads as needed.

Casa Rosita's Guacamole

Many friends rave about Rosita's famous restaurant in New York and the guacamole there. Here is my guacamole, based upon Rosita's version. It is delicious.

Makes 14 oz. or 6–8 servings

Ingredients

1 medium white, or 1 small Spanish, onion, chopped

5 oz. bunch fresh cilantro leaves

2 tsp. sea salt or kosher salt

4 garlic cloves, crushed

4 ripe Hass avocados

2 limes, halved, to garnish (optional)

2 green and 1 red chili, sliced

1/2 tsp. dried oregano (optional)

2 plum tomatoes, cut in 1/2 in. cubes

To serve:

Tostaditas, tortilla chips, warmed tortillas, torn

To prepare/make Using a big Mexican mortar (*molcahete*) or big mortar and pestle (or, less satisfactorily, a food-processor), combine the onion, cilantro, salt, and garlic and pound and mash, or process in brief bursts, to a green aromatic paste. Now scoop out and add the avocado flesh. Add a squeeze of fresh lime, if you like (Rosita does not do this), and the green chilies. Stir, pound, mix, or process briefly again. Crumble the oregano on top, if using (again, Rosita does not). Decorate with a tumble of red jewel-like tomato cubes and red chilies.

To present Serve surrounded by the lime halves and the tostaditas, tortilla chips, and torn tortilla pieces.

Salsa

Salsa cruda, generally of Mexican origin, means an uncooked sauce made from finely chopped savory ingredients with some acidity from citrus juice or vinegar. Some salsas contain oil; this one does not. It tastes fresh and lively. Hand chopped—not machine processed—salsas taste best.

Makes about 1 2/3 cups

Ingredients

I red onion, finely chopped

3 plum or vine tomatoes, finely cubed

2 hot fresh red or green chilies, deseeded, deveined, and chopped

juice of 2 limes or 1 lemon (5–6 tbsp.)

2 tbsp. stock or water

sea salt flakes and crushed allspice, to taste

1 handful fresh cilantro, mint, parsley, chives, or thyme, or a mix, chopped

To prepare/make Combine the ingredients in a nonreactive bowl, stirring. Taste, adjust seasonings as needed. Use the same day.

To present Serve in small or large bowls.

Variations

Substitute 3 scallions for the red onion.

Substitute blanched, dehusked tomatillos, or green tomatoes, for the red tomatoes.

Add 1 tsp. finely shredded fresh ginger and black pepper instead of allspice, and use all cilantro for an Asian-style salsa.

Add 3–4 tbsp. of extra-virgin olive oil for a richer effect.

Blini

with Taramasalata & Salmon "caviar"

Blini are yeast-risen pancakes, Russian in origin. Traditionally made of buckwheat, they are, these days, often made with part whole-wheat flour, part buckwheat flour, or even a hundred percent whole wheat flour. This recipe makes 48 blini, so freeze what you don't need for another occasion. Taramasalata, a Greek classic, should be made using pressed, salted cod's roe from a Greek deli. Substitute some salted, smoked cod's roe from a good fish market if none can be found, not authentic but good, even so. Time at a premium? Purchase ready-made blini, ready-made taramasalata, and add the salmon "caviar" as a garnish.

Makes 48
Allow 3–4 blini, 1 oz. taramasalata and 1 large tsp. salmon "caviar" per person for an appetizer; double this for a main course

Ingredients

Blini:

1 3/4 cups strong white bread flour

1/2 cup buckwheat flour

1 tsp. or 1/2 packet micronized easyblend yeast

1 tsp. sea salt flakes

1 cup milk, warmed to 90°F

2/3 cup sour cream

2 eggs, separated

6 tbsp. butter or olive oil, for cooking

Taramasalata:

4 tbsp. *tarama*: salted, pressed, cod's roe, or 4 oz. salted, smoked cod's roe, skinned, chopped

2 thick slices white bread, moistened and squeezed dry

2 garlic cloves, crushed

1 lemon

1 cup extra-virgin olive oil

3–4 tbsp. boiling water

handful fresh parsley, chopped

4 oz. jar salmon "caviar"

To prepare/cook blinis Sift together the flours, yeast, and salt in a large heat-resistant glass or ceramic bowl. Add the warmed milk, the sour cream, and the egg yolks, and lightly beat together to make a thick batter. Cover using a large plastic bag. Set on a rack over very warm water, not touching the bowl, or in another warm place. Leave for 40–50 minutes or until risen. Now whisk the egg whites to a stiff foam in a nonreactive bowl and fold in carefully. Preheat a large griddle, hot plate, nonstick or cast iron skillet. Add 1 tbsp. butter or olive oil. Spoon 8 tsp. of batter, from the tip of the spoon, to make small pancakes. Once the batter meets the hot surface it sets and bubbles will soon show on the uncooked upper surface. When this happens turn them over and cook again, briefly, until golden on the second side. Test one; it should be cooked right through. Cook the remaining batter in batches in more hot butter or olive oil. Cool on wire racks. Pack the cooled blini, in stacks, in a cloth-lined little basket or box for transporting.

To prepare taramasalata Put the *tarama* or smoked cod's roe into a food-processor with the wet, crumbled bread, the garlic, and juice of half the lemon. Process briefly until mixed. Now, with the machine running, drizzle in the oil, in a thin, fine stream until the mixture stiffens into a dense paste. Scrape down the sides as necessary. Now drizzle in 3–4 tbsp. of boiling water (or more as needed) with the machine running, to lighten the texture. Throw in the parsley and stop the machine. Pack the finished taramasalata into a medium-sized china or shatterproof glass jar or pot with a lid. If necessary wrap in plastic wrap or a wet cloth for transporting.

To present Set out the blini, opened taramasalata, and the opened salmon "caviar" with the remaining lemon half. Have small knives ready for spreading.

Mini Game Burgers

with Bacon

Delicious, gamey meat patties with juniper and Armagnac to accentuate the autumnal tastes. They are just the thing for a harvest picnic.

Makes 1 3/4 lb., 16 burgers
Allow 2 burgers per serving as an appetizer

Ingredients

6 1/2 oz. boneless, skinless duck or pheasant, in 1/2 in. cubes

9 oz. smoked bacon

4 tbsp. Armagnac

6 tbsp. chopped fresh herbs, e.g., parsley, rosemary, thyme, or oregano

1 small onion, finely chopped

salt and freshly ground black pepper

12 oz. ground beef or veal

1 cup fresh bread crumbs

2 tsp. juniper berries, crushed

1 egg, beaten

2 tbsp. extra-virgin olive oil

To prepare/cook Put the diced game into a nonreactive bowl. Reserve half the bacon; finely scissor-cut or grind the rest, and add to the bowl. Add the Armagnac, and the herbs, onion, and the seasonings. Marinate for 20 minutes, or several hours in the refrigerator, then stir in the ground meat, bread crumbs, crushed juniper berries, and the egg. Mix well, kneading with clean hands to make a dense meat paste. Stretch each reserved bacon slice using a knife blade, and halve lengthwise. Divide the meat into 16 equal portions. Squeeze each portion tightly into a ball then flatten into a burger about 2 in. across. Wrap a bacon slice around the outer edge. Hold it in place with a wooden toothpick. Repeat until all are prepared. Heat the oil in a large heavy-based or nonstick skillet. Add the burgers and sauté over medium-high heat for 3–4 minutes on the first side, and 2–3 minutes on the second. The burgers should be slightly rosy inside, but if you prefer, cook them longer until done to your liking. Remove the toothpicks.

To present Serve hot, warm, or cold (but not chilled) with scallions or salad leaves of the season. Eat using the hands or with a knife and fork.

Pork Rillettes

with Endive and Rolls

Rillettes resemble pâté but the meat is cooked slowly in seasoned fat before being shredded and packed into small jars. Make them at least one day ahead; they keep, refrigerated and well sealed, for weeks. If you wish, substitute up to a third of the pork with pickled belly pork in place of fresh, or with duck, goose, rabbit, or hare.

Makes about 1³/₄ lb., Serves 8

Ingredients

3¹/₄ lb. belly pork, including rind, or boneless pork chops with fat

4 garlic cloves

¹/₂ nutmeg, grated (1 tsp. grated nutmeg)

1–2 tbsp. black peppercorns, coarsely crushed

1¹/₂–2 tbsp. sea salt flakes or kosher salt

3 oz. bunch parsley stalks, tied with string

3–4 bay leaves

2 oz. fresh thyme sprigs, plus extra to garnish

To serve:

8 crusty bread rolls

1 head Belgian endive or a handful of arugula leaves

To prepare/cook Remove the pork rind in one piece and any bones and cartilage, and set aside. Now chop the meat into 1 in. chunks. Put the rind, fat side down, in the base of a flameproof casserole. Add the meat, bones, cartilage, and remaining ingredients. Pour in 7 tbsp. of cold water; cover tightly. Bring the pan contents to a simmer, check, cover tightly again and turn to the lowest possible heat, or put into a low oven preheated to 250°F. Cook, undisturbed, for about 3 hours until the meat and fat disintegrate. Do not let the pan boil dry; add a few tbsp. of water, as needed, now and then to prevent any signs of frying. Remove casserole from the heat. Pour contents into a sieve over a bowl. Discard rind, bones, cartilage, any other debris such as bay leaves and stems. Using two forks, tease apart and shred the solids. Put in a clean bowl. Add enough of the strained fat to create a creamy paste. Smooth the mixture into one large or several small ramekins. Drizzle over extra fat, thinly, to seal. Push reserved thyme sprigs into the fat to garnish. Once the rillettes are completely cold, refrigerate. Add lids or tops after several hours of chilling. Take the ramekins to your site.

To present Let people help themselves; scoop the rillettes into each split roll to make a thick layer and push in some Belgian endive or arugula leaves. (If the rolls are made ahead, wrap them in waxed paper).

Smoked Salmon Fritters

Smoked salmon, cooked rice, seasonings, and eggs combine to make golden and puffy fritters to eat as finger food, and is easy to transport. They are good cool rather than chilled. Fold each in little romaine leaves before eating. Go to an Asian deli for *wasabi* powder.

Makes 24, Serves 8

Ingredients

4 1/2 oz. smoked salmon, scissor-cut

4 1/2 oz. cooked white or brown long grain rice or wild rice

6 scallions, chopped

1/2 tsp. *wasabi* powder

3 tbsp. tomato juice

2 eggs, separated

sea salt and freshly ground black pepper

4 tbsp. extra-virgin olive oil

To serve:

limes and romaine leaves

To prepare/cook Combine the smoked salmon, rice, scallions, *wasabi*, tomato juice, and egg yolks in a bowl, stirring with a fork. Do not mash. In a small separate high-sided bowl whisk the egg whites with a pinch of the salt to stiff peaks. Fold this into the salmon-rice mixture with about 1 tsp. of salt, and pepper to taste. Heat 1 tbsp. of the oil in a nonstick or heavy-based skillet. Spoon in 6 small portions (about a tbsp. each) of mixture. Reduce the heat to low. Cook until golden and crusty, 1 1/2–2 minutes on each side. Test one; it must be cooked right through. Repeat with more oil until you have finished the mixture (total of 4 batches). Cool the fritters to room temperature. Chill them if they are to travel far. Pack the washed lettuce leaves separately, wrapped in wet paper towels with some ice cubes. Enclose in a plastic bag or box. Pack the cool fritters in another box.

To present Wrap each fritter in a few lettuce leaves, squeeze a little lime juice over, and eat with your hands.

Smoked Trout Pâté

with Celery

Forget those heavy, dense pâtés crusted with butter and laden with fat; this one is as fresh and clean as a new spring day. Make it in minutes and serve in one big, or several little ramekins. Chill it well or even freeze it briefly before you set out.

Makes about 12 oz., Serves 8
Allow about 2 oz. per serving

Ingredients

9 oz. boneless, skinless hot-smoked trout

1 tsp. extra-virgin olive oil

2 garlic cloves, chopped

1 tbsp. lemon juice

1/2 cup cream cheese or low-fat soft cheese

1–2 tsp. mild paprika

sea salt and freshly ground black pepper

2 tbsp. chopped fresh herbs e.g. dill, chives

2 celery hearts

To prepare/make Flake the trout into a food-processor or large mortar. Heat the olive oil in a skillet and sauté the garlic briefly. Add the lemon juice. Spoon this in with the trout and process, or pound using a pestle. Add the soft cheese, paprika, seasonings, and some of the herbs and process, in brief bursts, or pound briefly, to make a pale pink paste, with a slightly rough texture. Taste and adjust seasonings. Smooth into one large or several small, lidded metal containers or ramekins. Push a little fresh herb on top of each, and a little extra black pepper. Chill for 1 hour, or refrigerate for up to 4 days. Briefly freeze—say for 45 minutes—if the weather is hot and the journey long. Wash and shake dry the celery. Wrap it in wet paper towels or cloth and plastic. Chill it while the pâté chills. Take a knife for spreading.

To present Surround the trout pâté with some crisp, freshly cut lengths of celery.

Soups

Soups are suddenly having a renaissance and are, once again, funky and fun. "Big bowl" cafés serving dumplings and noodles in hot broth, and juice bars which serve freshly squeezed juices and smoothies (reminiscent of iced fruit soups) can be seen as part of the same story. Soup is back in fashion again.

Hot soup is a salvation to anyone feeling cold, discouraged, and in need of a boost. But ethnic, epicurean, chilled, sweet, and even jellied soups exist as well; the scope is enormous and infinitely interesting. And soup is easily portable.

Gazpacho, bouillabaisse, congee, caldo verde, consommé; such names summon up real magnificence. All of these are soups, all of them are famous. They sustain people the world over.

Be bold with whatever soup you serve. Soup should arrive very hot or icy cold. Few soups taste ideal when lukewarm, so pack and organize accordingly. These days, with vacuum flasks, insulated containers, and excellent cooking apparatus good for picnics, snack meals, and barbecues, it's become easy to exploit their possibilities.

Apply the same creativity to the size of your soup servings; tiny cups, glasses, or miniature china bowls can be perfect for certain soups. Others deserve to be presented in giant mugs, big earthy cups, generous bowls, or heat-resistant glass tumblers.

The recipe ideas mentioned so far can be a basis for your own exploration. The favorite recipes found in this book include iced black bean soup with chipotle cream; carrot, orange, and cardamom soup; borscht; green pea and prosciutto soup. You will also find miso soup containing *dashi* with noodles in the bento picnic box. These soups have flavor, color, and in some cases, unusual textures. There is the fresh boost of chili, herbs, or spices, or the sweet scent of prosciutto to add appeal. Although some of the soups are here served hot, you could equally well serve them cold.

Soups are very versatile, as long as you taste and season intelligently and garnish them appropriately. But if you want them elegant, or subtle, they can satisfy these requirements too. Of all the dishes in this book, these are some of the most easily made and easily enjoyed.

Enjoy soups alone—as a feast in their own right, accompanied by some crusty bread and followed by fresh fruit—or as part of the menus suggested later.

Carrot, Orange, & Cardamom Soup

An exotic, colorful and fragrant soup which can be made in a flash. Serve it hot or iced. The harissa, a red, spicy, North African condiment, is delicious when homemade (see page 69) and is also available at some gourmet shops.

Makes 5 cups, Serves 4

Ingredients

1 1/4 lb. large organic carrots, peeled and thinly sliced

3 cups chicken or vegetable stock, boiling

1/2 tsp. sea salt flakes

1–2 tsp. harissa (hot spicy) paste

20 green cardamom pods, crushed, plus 8 to garnish

2 oranges, scrubbed

1 small shallot, finely chopped

To prepare/cook Put the carrots in a small saucepan. Add the hot stock, bring to a boil, and reduce to a lively simmer. Add the salt, harissa, and black cardamom seeds removed from their green pods. Stir to mix. Now squeeze in the juice of the oranges. Use a grater or zester to remove 1/4–1/2 tsp. of orange zest. Once the carrots are tender, 10–12 minutes, allow to cool and then pour the pan contents plus the zest and shallot into a blender. Blend to a creamy soup. Heat to boiling, or chill thoroughly. Pour the soup into a vacuum flask and seal. Wrap up the extra cardamom pods and take along as well.

To present Use bowls, cups, or glasses for serving the soup. Scatter on some extra cardamom seeds for garnish just before serving.

Green Pea & Prosciutto Soup

Real, fresh baby green peas in the pod are a brief luxury; they must be eaten within hours of picking. This recipe, using easily obtainable frozen *petits pois*, gives you the sweetness, color, succulence, and vitamins of fresh peas and it can be completed within 20 minutes. Serve it hot or cold, with some mellow cured Italian ham added at the end.

Makes 6 1/4 cups, Serves 8

Ingredients

2 tbsp. butter, chopped

6 scallions, green and white parts, sliced

2 oz. new potatoes, scrubbed and sliced

6 cups frozen petits pois

2 1/2 cups boiling water

1 cup whole milk

6 thin slices prosciutto

salt and freshly ground white pepper

To prepare/cook Heat the butter in a saucepan and when sizzling add the scallions and sliced potatoes. Fry for 1–2 minutes, stirring now and then. Add the peas and boiling water and bring the pan contents back to a boil. Cover the pan, reduce heat and cook for 8 minutes more. Add half the milk and half the pan contents to a blender. Blend until smooth. Pour out the blended soup. Now, to the blender, add the remaining milk, remaining pan contents, and 2 of the ham slices, scissor-cut. Blend again until smooth. Combine the two mixtures, stir, taste, and season well. Reheat to boiling once again and pour into wide-mouthed vacuum flask and seal. Alternatively chill completely, then add several ice cubes and pour into the vacuum flask. Wrap the remaining prosciutto in waxed paper.

To present Pour out the soup, hot or cold, into big mugs, china cups, or soup bowls. Pass soup spoons. Shred the remaining prosciutto into each serving.

Iced Black Bean Soup

with Chipotle Cream

A Mexican-style soup and a beauty. If authentic dried black beans are hard to find, substitute several cans of good quality black beans instead, this saves hours.

Makes 6¼ cups, Serves 8

Ingredients

4 tbsp. corn oil

8 scallions, chopped

4 garlic cloves, crushed

1 green jalapeño chili, cored, deseeded, sliced

1 tsp. ground cumin

2 tsp. ground coriander

3 oz. fresh cilantro, chopped

2 tbsp. tomato purée

1 lb. 10 oz. cooked or canned black beans *(frijoles negros)*

3 cups boiling chicken stock

sea salt and freshly ground black pepper

To serve:

2 tbsp. chipotles in brine, or dried chipotles (smoked, dried jalapeños)

½ cup heavy cream

To prepare/cook Heat the oil, add the scallions and sauté 2–3 minutes. Now add the garlic, green jalapeño, cumin, ground coriander, fresh cilantro, tomato purée, and beans. Pour in the boiling stock. Bring the pan contents back to boiling. Simmer, uncovered, for 15 minutes or so. Blend the soup using a blender or immersion blender, in batches if necessary, until creamy. Return the soup to the pan. Stir, adjust seasonings and turn off the heat. Cool the soup over iced water. Chill in the refrigerator. Make the chipotle cream: if using chipotles in brine simply chop or mash. If using dried chipotles, dry roast them briefly in a hot skillet, soak briefly in hot water, simmer until soft, and chop or mash. Stir into the cream and pack separately. Once the soup is cold, pour into one or two wide-mouthed vacuum flasks, adding 2 ice cubes to each.

To present Stir the chipotle cream into the soup at serving time.

Hot Borscht

with Rolls or Bagels

The best borscht I've tasted was in Moscow; the next best in Paris, but my own version is decidedly tasty. Raw beets work best; if unobtainable use canned beets. Serve this soup with sour cream, crème fraîche or, more abstemiously, with low-fat fromage frais. Rolls or bagels are a great accompaniment.

Makes 6½ cups, Serves 8

Ingredients

1 tbsp. virgin olive oil

4 garlic cloves, chopped or crushed

1 red onion, sliced

⅛–¼ fresh red chili, e.g. serrano, or habanero

1 carrot, thinly sliced

¼ oz. dried mushrooms e.g. ceps or morels, crumbled

1 lb. 5 oz. fresh beets or cooked canned beets

4 cups boiling chicken stock

2–3 tbsp. red wine vinegar

salt and freshly ground black pepper

handful fresh cilantro leaves, to garnish

To serve:

8 tbsp. sour cream, cream or low-fat fromage frais

8 crusty white rolls or bagels

To prepare/cook Combine the oil, garlic, onion, chili, carrot, and mushrooms in a saucepan. Cook, stirring, over high heat for 2 minutes. Peel, slice or cube the beets into the pan then add the boiling stock, and most of the vinegar. Bring the pan contents back to boiling. Reduce heat, simmer for 15–20 minutes or until the beets are tender and flavors blended. Taste, add remaining vinegar if you like, and add salt and pepper to balance. (If you prefer a smooth soup, blend the soup to a purée). Pour the hot soup into a wide-mouthed vacuum flask. Seal tightly. Pack the herbs and cream or sour cream separately in jars with secure lids. Pack cups, mugs, glasses, or bowls.

To present Pour out portions of soup. Add a spoonful of cream, sour cream, or fromage frais, and sprinkle with cilantro leaves. Pass the rolls or bagels and enjoy.

Sandwiches & wraps

Food put between slices of bread, or rolled up inside salad leaves, flatbreads, or rice-paper wraps can be really fun, truly portable, multicultural, and completely delectable. It goes without saying that the ingredients must be at peak freshness; the salad leaves crisp, the seafood, meat, or poultry perfect. Flavored butters and spreads can add interest, good seasoning mixes or dressings give finesse.

Watercress Sandwiches *page 43*

Pa Am Tomaquet *page 46*

Lebanese Lamb Wraps *page 48*

A roll and some soup, bread and cheese, salad and some fresh fruit; these must be some of the best-known, and well-loved quick snacks, easily carried to another place. Food on the move; a sandwich could be said to be a perfect example of this. Yet, oddly, sandwiches are often consigned to the footnotes of cooking, not taken very seriously. This seems a pity; they are an eminently useful idea, and can be as exciting, and varied as any main course dish.

There are hundreds of sandwich formats; from bruschetta to *bocadillos*—versions of which are included in this chapter. Sandwiches may be open or closed, small or large. They can be made using long French bread sticks or round crusty loaves, flat focaccia or ciabatta loaves, sourdough "subs," wholegrain rolls; the list is endless. They may be hearty or refined, spicy or mild.

Flat, layered sandwiches are not the only type; rolled-up sandwiches are a stylish alternative; a common sense solution to eating on the run, using hands, not forks. Such roll-ups and wraps are found in the Middle East, in South East Asia, and many other areas. The wrappers may be made of thin, flatbreads such as pita bread; they may be made of flour tortillas. Sometimes the wraps are made of salad leaves for freshness. These may combine melon, peach, or avocado with spicy or savory foods; cured ham or hummus, for example, to create contrast and variety.

The best sandwiches are often created on site, using fresh bread split open and whatever local specialty—cheeses, pickles, pâtés, spicy vegetable spreads—is available and excellent. Some of these ideas are incorporated in Chapter 1.

Spreads matter, too, in sandwich making. Fresh butter, lovely olive oil, spreadable soft cheeses all work well. I have included several ideas for you to make your own flavored butters.

If the chunkier breads are to be toasted or grilled, this must be done quickly, keeping the outside crisp, the inner crumb still soft. Drizzle on estate-bottled extra-virgin olive oil for the best flavor.

Try to avoid using the kind of "factory" breads which taste of nothing, or soften to a pulp. Choose crusty bread from your local bakery, or delicious ethnic breads. Next, have herbs and salads crisp, well-drained, and cold; meats and seafood, egg products, cheeses, and rice should be at the best, appropriate, safe temperature.

Depending upon the situation, packing, wrapping or organizing "make-on-the-spot" wraps and sandwiches need a little care and attention, so follow the lively suggestions here for good results, and enjoy these convenient and delicious portable feasts.

FLAVORED BUTTERS

Throughout this book you'll find flavored butters—such the barbecue baste used with the shrimp cooked for a beach barbecue, truffle butter (to go on hot noodles), and a butter "mousse." You will find chutney butter (with the ham and gherkin roll-ups) and ginger and citrus butter (part of crab and ginger sandwiches); use these according to your own ideas.

You can also buy a range of flavored ready-made butters—such as garlic and herb butter—and butter itself comes in many varieties: salted, mildly salted, unsalted.

Butter, used wisely, can boost the flavors and it means that your sandwiches are well stuck together when in transit.

Here is a list of ready-made items which, beaten into a little softened butter, will be delicious additions to your picnic or portable feast:

Pesto, tapenade, sun-dried tomato paste, purées of garlic, lemongrass, or ginger; anchovies (mashed to a paste), capers (chopped and mashed), grated parmesan or cheddar, herbed cheese, blue cheese. Easiest of all, freshly crushed garlic and whatever herbs are in season. Even peanut butter, with a shake of chili sauce and soy sauce, some softened butter, and a few chopped scallions or shreds of ginger, can make plain flatbreads delectable. Or add crumbled crisp bacon; peanut butter and bacon is delicious.

Experiment with flavored butters—and create interest and curiosity among your guests.

Cheese, Ham, & Salad-filled Mini Loaves

These are masterpieces of invention; fillings packed neatly into crusty rolls or tiny loaves with the top lids and crumb removed. The lid is then set back on top, sealing them for traveling. To eat they can be sliced into halves or quarters.

Serves 4

Ingredients

4 round or oval crusty rolls

6 tbsp. extra-virgin olive oil

4 tbsp. fresh pesto (not pasteurized)

1 handful flatleaf parsley, chopped

8 slices prosciutto

9 oz. canned, roasted artichokes
or wild mushrooms in oil, drained

4 1/2 oz. soft blue cheese

16 dry-cured salted black olives, pitted,
or anchovy-stuffed green olives

To prepare Slice off and keep the lids of each roll. Set aside. Using a grapefruit knife, scoop out the crumbs, leaving an even, crusty wall or shell. Pile the crumbs into a food-processor along with half the olive oil, the pesto, and parsley. Process in bursts to get densely green crumbs. Use the remaining oil to brush inside each hollowed-out roll, including the inside of the lid. Spoon an eighth of the crumbs into each roll. Add a folded prosciutto slice. Add more crumbs, and a quarter of the roasted artichokes or mushrooms, and cheese. Push in the second prosciutto slice and 4 olives. Push the lid into place on top. Wrap tightly using waxed paper, plastic wrap, or dampened cloth. Wedge them, upright, into a small box or basket.

To present Undo the wrappings. Let diners eat them whole, halved, or quartered.

Crusty Breads

with Spicy Peppers & Spanish Ham

This is a well-loved snack in Spain where it is called a *bocadillo*, or "little mouthful." The tastes are delightful: the olive oil is invariably fruity and spicy, the cured meats superb and the pickles, preserves, and beans wonderful. Drink a classy full-bodied red wine to complete the image.

Serves 4

Ingredients

4 bread rolls, about 6 in. long

5 tbsp. extra-virgin olive oil

9 oz. cooked white beans (canned, or in jars from
a good delicatessen)

4 garlic cloves, crushed

salt and freshly ground black pepper

8 thin slices Spanish cured ham (*jamon serrano*)

8–12 canned *piquillo* peppers (roasted, skinned,
spicy red peppers) or canned pimientos

To prepare Slice the rolls lengthwise almost in two but keep a hinge on each. Drizzle the interior crumb of each base with 2 tsp. of the oil, almost 3 tbsp. in total. Mash 2 tbsp. of the remaining oil with the white beans, garlic, salt, and pepper, to make a paste. Spoon a quarter of this bean paste along each roll. Fold in 2 slices of ham to each. Pack 2 or 3 *piquillo* peppers on top. Now wrap each roll in a square of waxed paper or a colorful cloth. Pack into a basket or bag to carry.

To present Unwrap and eat.

Ham & Gherkin Roll-ups

Sweet, cooked ham, sharply piquant baby gherkins, and chutney-flavored butter, all rolled up inside soft white bread makes finger food which is easy and delicious. These roll-ups are also extremely convenient to pack.

Makes 16, Serves 4

Ingredients

8 thin slices very fresh white bread (square loaf)

2 tbsp. salted butter, softened

1 tbsp. mango or other chutney, finely chopped

24 tiny cocktail baby gherkins or 1 large dill pickle, drained

8 slices cooked smoked ham

To prepare Put the bread slices in a pile. Use a sharp, serrated knife to slice off and discard the crusts. Wrap the bread briefly in a dampened cloth, or spray with water. Meanwhile mix the soft butter with the chutney. Drain and dry the gherkins. If using a large dill pickle, slice lengthwise into 8. Unwrap the bread; line the slices up in a row. Using a spatula, rubber scraper, or palette knife, coat the bread slices with the chutney-butter. Put each bread slice on a square of plastic wrap, and set a ham slice on each. Put 3 gherkins (end to end) or a dill pickle segment diagonally across each ham-covered bread slice. Now, starting at one corner, roll each slice up tightly. Place these, seam side down, on the same dampened cloth, in two piles. Wrap up neatly. Pack inside a plastic box or bag. Take a sharp, folding knife.

To present Cut across, at an angle, giving 16 roll-ups, and remove plastic wrap.

Watercress Sandwiches

Somehow this brings to mind childhood simplicity.
Ensure that the watercress is very clean, the butter at a
spreading temperature, and the bread soft.

Makes 24 small sandwiches, Serves 4

Ingredients

12 thin slices white bread (square loaf)

6 tbsp. salted butter, softened

2 tbsp. thick mayonnaise

2 tsp. boiling water

1 bunch or 2 packs watercress or cress, washed

freshly ground black pepper

To prepare/make Spread out the bread into two rows, edges touching, so
that it makes one rectangle. Whisk the butter with the mayonnaise, and the
boiling water; you should obtain a mousse-like cream. Use a wide-bladed
spatula or rubber scraper to smooth the butter-mousse across all the bread
slices, right to the edges. Shake the cress dry. Pull or snip off the watercress
sprigs and press them on the buttered surfaces of half the slices so they are
well covered. Sprinkle with black pepper to taste. Lay a buttered slice face
down on a watercress-covered slice; pile up the sandwiches into a tower.
Pressing down evenly, use a sharp, serrated knife to slice off and discard the
crusts. Leave the sandwiches whole. Use waxed paper, plastic wrap, or a wet
cotton cloth to wrap the sandwiches tightly in a neat block. Take the same
sharp, serrated knife to the picnic site along with a lettuce, washed and
wrapped in dampened cloth or plastic.

To present Unwrap the sandwiches. Slice into four triangles, squares, or
fingers. Arrange as liked on a plate, basket, or tray.

Crab & Ginger Sandwiches

I first tasted these at a party. We sipped wine, and a waiter carried around a handsome sourdough loaf, inside which, like treasures, we found tiny little sandwiches. You can vary the filling but keep the idea; it's impressive, portable, and certainly a stylish feast.

Serves 8 or more

Ingredients

1 large round sourdough or whole-wheat loaf (about 2 lb.)

1 lemon or lime

6 tbsp. salted butter, softened

1 in. piece fresh ginger, scrubbed

14 oz. prepared, cooked crabmeat, lobster, or smoked salmon

3 tbsp. thick mayonnaise

1/8 tsp. cayenne pepper

sea salt and freshly ground black pepper

To prepare Slice off a top "lid" from the loaf; set it aside. Using a short, sharp, serrated knife, make a vertical cut, about 1/2 in. in from the crust, all the way round and nearly to the base. Cut a line across the center of the crumb to make two semicircles. Using your hands, carefully lift out a semicircular "plug" of bread. Repeat on the other side. Trim the bases of these bread chunks to make them smooth. Turn the pieces of crumb flat side down, and, using a carving knife or long sharp, serrated knife, slice each thinly into 6 or 8 thin layers. Stack in 2 piles, in the shape of the original chunks, and cover with a dampened cloth. Squeeze a little lemon or lime and finely grate a little zest into the butter. Using a fine metal grater, grate the ginger, skin and all. Scrape the pulp into the butter. In a bowl, break up the crabmeat with a fork, add the mayonnaise and seasonings. Beat well until smooth. Unwrap the bread. Butter 2 bread slices and spread on a share of crab filling. Press the sandwich closed. Repeat until all the bread, butter, and filling are used up, and wrap once again in the damp cloth for 10–30 minutes. Unwrap. Stack the finished sandwiches in the same chunks again, and insert each carefully in the hollow loaf. Slice the sandwiches across, inside the hollowed-out loaf crust, to make quarters, and again to make triangles. Set the lid on top of the loaf. Wrap the entire loaf in plastic wrap or foil.

To present On site, unwrap the loaf and place on a cloth-covered tray. Allow friends to lift the lid and help themselves.

Pa Am Tomaquet

In northern Spain, this famous and delicious snack seems as usual as pizza does in Italy. It consists of local produce: chunky bread, grilled, rubbed with a smashed garlic clove, then with a crushed ripe tomato. Salt is usually added, but the final flourish is a generous drizzle of extra-virgin olive oil; a tomato sandwich which is a triumph of simplicity, ease, and freshness. This can be created on site, as long as there is a barbecue.

Serves 4

Ingredients

4 thick slices from a crusty country loaf

4 garlic cloves, skin on

4 large ripe, juicy tomatoes

sea salt

extra-virgin olive oil, for drizzling

To prepare Get the barbecue to the heated temperature. Toast the bread, both sides, over the heat. Crush each garlic clove and use it to rub garlic all over one side of the toast. Now rub squashy tomato flesh over too; if it looks pink and messy, that's par for the course. Add salt to taste and a generous trickle of oil.

To present Eat each sandwich while warm and crusty. Add more salt and oil to the leftover tomato and eat that too.

Sheep's Cheese on Bruschetta

Long before bruschetta became fashionable it was a peasant dish from Italy, designed to maximize the pleasure of tasting the new season's olive oil. Chunks of homely bread are toasted or chargrilled briefly then rubbed with garlic and sprinkled lavishly with the best olive oil available. In this version, pecorino is added. Some fresh greens—watercress, or arugula—can also be added.

Serves 4

Ingredients

4 thick slices Italian-style bread

4 garlic cloves, squashed

extra-virgin olive oil, to taste

9 oz. pecorino cheese or other sheep's cheese

fresh greens such as watercress, or rocket (optional)

sea salt

To prepare On site, fire up a portable barbecue, or make a small wood fire (if it is safe). Barbecue or toast the bread on a rack over the heat. Use the garlic to rub all over one side of the crusty bread, then drizzle on oil. Add some slices of cheese and some fresh greens. Sprinkle with salt to taste.

To present Hand around the ready-made open sandwiches.

Lebanese Lamb Wraps

These little lamb meatballs hail from the Middle East where they are called *kibbeh*. They traditionally contain cracked wheat, but I use couscous which adds an interesting texture. Kibbeh are delicious served hot, but are also wonderful served warm or even at room temperature for your picnic. Flour tortillas or pita bread can be used to make the wraps.

Serves 4

Ingredients

1 lb. twice-ground good quality lean lamb

2 tbsp. spice mix such as "Ali Berbère" (see page 68)

1 tsp. celery salt

1 handful parsley, chopped

2/3 cup "instant" couscous

7 tbsp. boiling stock or water

2 garlic cloves, chopped

2 tbsp. freshly squeezed lemon juice

1 handful fresh mint, chopped

To serve:

4 thin tortillas or pita breads

1/2 cup presoaked, pitted dried apricots

extra flatleaf parsley sprigs

8–12 romaine lettuce leaves (outer ones)

1/2 cup chickpea and tahini paste (*hummus bi tahini*) (see page 22) (optional)

To prepare/cook Mix the lamb, spice mix, celery salt, and parsley together. Leave to stand, covered, in a cool place. Mix the couscous with the boiling stock, garlic, lemon juice, and, once it has cooled, the mint. Leave until cold. Drain off any excess liquid. Then add the lamb and knead it all well together. Divide into 12. Shape each into a torpedo-shaped *kibbeh*, smoothing off the ends. Cook these by baking in an oven preheated to 350°F for 20–25 minutes or microwave them, 6 at a time, on High (750 watts) for 3 minutes, turning them over after 2 minutes. If you prefer, broil (8–10 minutes, turning) or barbecue (about 10 minutes). Pack in foil to remain warm, or allow to cool to room temperature before packing.

To present Wrap each *kibbeh* in a wrap of flat bread, adding some apricot halves, parsley, romaine leaves, and a dollop, if you like, of ready-made *hummus bi tahini*.

Prosciutto & Radicchio Wraps

These are a miracle of ease and style. Select crisp, pretty Italian salad leaves. Keep them intact and, on site, roll them up around a twist of fine fragrant prosciutto, one of the world's most delicious of foods, and some freshly sliced melon, such as cantaloupe.

Serves 4–6

Ingredients
4 heads red radicchio
12 slices prosciutto
1 ripe, scented canteloupe
fresh peppercorns, in a pepper grinder

To prepare/make
Separate and wash the radicchio leaves. Leave the prosciutto on its waxed paper, rolled up loosely. Cut up the melon in slivers, removing skin and seeds. Pack in transportable containers.

To present
On site, set out all the components in a cloth-lined hamper or basket and add a pile of plates. Participants take one or two leaves of radicchio, add a slice of ham, a slivor of melon, and a few grinds of pepper. It is then rolled up and eaten.

Vietnamese Rice-paper Wraps

These delicacies are best assembled on the spot by each person. Take along the packet of rice-paper sheets, a flask of warm water to soften them, the fillings, and the dips. Duck breast scented with 5-spice powder, crisp raw vegetables, and fresh mint go inside. Salted peanut garnish and one or two dips complete the dish. Making these snacks is fun—have them as thin or as well-filled as you like.

Serves 6

Ingredients

2 smoked duck breast halves

1 tsp. 5-spice powder

1 tsp. dark soy sauce

1 x 12 oz. pack triangular or round Vietnamese rice wrappers (*Bahn Trang*)

Fillings and serving stuffs:

1 carrot, in long shreds

4 scallions, in long shreds

9 oz. daikon radish, peeled, in long strips

1/2 cup bean sprouts

2 red bell peppers, deseeded, in long strips

1 cup fresh mint

1 romaine lettuce, washed but whole

1/2 cup hoisin sauce, yellow bean sauce, or plum sauce

1/2 cup roasted, salted peanuts, chopped

1/2 cup sweet chili sauce (Chinese type)

1/2 cup *nuoc cham* sauce (see page 99)

To prepare/cook Rub the smoked duck breasts all over with the spice powder, and the soy. Bake in an oven preheated to 400°F for 30–40 minutes or until brown and juicy. Wet the salad fillings slightly (to ensure they remain crisp), and pack along with the lettuce into a large plastic container or similar item. Pack the hoisin sauce, peanuts, chili sauce, and *nuoc cham* into small, separate tubs or bowls. Keep the rice wrappers dry and separated. Slice or shred the cooked, smoked duck into yet another sealed container, or foil. Take a vacuum flask of warm water for softening the rice wrappers, also an unbreakable dish or bowl and a pastry brush.

To present Unwrap and display all the various ingredients. Pour out the warm water into the bowl for the diners to dip and soften each rice wrap. The alternative is to paint one side with water, using a pastry brush, until it softens. Shake each one free from drips. Take a lettuce leaf as a plate and place a wrapper on it. Spread the wrap with some hoisin, yellow bean sauce, or plum sauce. Add some duck then some salad stuffs. Roll up the wrap, tucking in the ends if you like. Now dip each wrap first into a dipping sauce, then into some peanuts. Eat it; leaf "plate," wrap, and all. Continue until all ingredients have been used up.

Barbecue

"Let's have a barbecue!" This always seems a welcome invitation. Images of relaxed conversation, warm midday sun, or the gentle fading light of dusk, with a refreshing drink in your hand and the enticing smell of smoke, the sizzle as food cooks, all seem utterly appealing.

Mexican barbecue *page 56*

Clambake *page 60*

Country barbecue *page 64*

Outdoor cooking over a wood or charcoal fire is about the most ancient of cooking methods. It lends to the cooked food a uniquely appetite-arousing, smoky savor. It also arouses a sense of adventure.

Barbecues are an easy way to entertain a number of people in a relaxed and informal way.

Outdoor cooking can happen in many different ways, from convenient portable gas grills, tiny hibachis for one or two people, simple kettle grills, or even outdoor stone ovens which can roast or barbecue.

Barbecue disasters mainly stem from the lack of understanding that the best grilling is done once the flames have died down and the embers are at a steady, gentle, ashy glow. Barbecuing and grilling takes patience, so have a selection of delicious snacks and drinks to sip while you wait. Anticipation sharpens the appetite!

Setting the food an appropriate distance from the heat—so that the inside cooks in the time it takes to sizzle, but not char the exterior—is the other important consideration.

Another concern is that sugary glazes and marinades, though often tasty, can cook too quickly and become too dark. Use these recipes as a basic guide and do not overdo things. Evenly sized food also helps to make the cooking process error-free. Pounding some foods may help; sometimes threading foods on to skewers is the best solution to ensure even cooking.

When grilling, be careful not to overly char the food, but also ensure the food is properly cooked through, for both taste and health purposes. Another safely issue: always have a hose, water, fire extinguisher, or fire blanket on hand when grilling.

Check that the metal parts of any barbecue are of chrome-plated steel and rust-resistant. Pack suitable foods, prepared and raw, lots of hot and cold drinks, packs of ice in insulated containers, kitchen paper, napkins, charcoal, your portable barbecue (or the makings for your wood fire), tools, and then be off. Cushions, umbrellas, and some sunscreen are important too.

Mexican barbecue

Mexico has a vivid appeal. Revel in some of its spicy, herbal chili-enhanced flavors, its earthy, colorful dishes, and its easy conviviality by creating this barbecue or *parilla* menu. Add some margaritas, open some beers, hang up paper lanterns, and light candles; it's fiesta time.

Chicken Fajitas

with Salad

Fajitas—traditionally made with strips of beef in a marinade—are made with wheat, not corn tortillas and are a favorite at any gathering. This cross-cultural version uses chicken. For a beach barbecue (*parilla*) for a crowd make it simple. These fajitas are do-it-yourself; this makes it fun for all and not merely hardwork for the cooks. The four-skewer system for holding the quickly-cooked chicken is foolproof; try it. There is no waiting as all the chicken is ready at the same time.

Serves 8

Ingredients

1 lb. can pinto beans, mashed

1 cup barbecue sauce

2 1/2 cups guacamole (see page 22) or bought guacamole

scant 2 cups sour cream

2 cups low-fat soft cheese or farmer's cheese, crumbled or sliced

16 whole wheat tortillas

2 tsp. fresh red chili, sliced

6 tbsp. sun-dried tomato paste or tomatillo purée

4 tbsp. corn oil

8 boneless chicken breast halves, each sliced lengthwise into 6

1 large handful fresh cilantro leaves

4 fresh limes, in chunky pieces

To prepare/cook Mash the drained pinto beans, either before you set out or on site, in their can using a fork, and adding the barbecue-tomato sauce to make a thick bean purée. Put the mashed pinto beans, guacamole, sour cream, and the cheese in separate bowls or containers which can be passed around. Have the tortillas covered, maybe in baskets or between cloths, near to the grill ready for being warmed and filled.

To make the coating for the chicken, mix the chopped fresh red chili together with the tomato paste or tomatillo purée, mixing in the corn oil. Toss the chicken strips in the chili mixture until coated. Line up 24 chicken strips in a parallel row. Using 2 long skewers, thread the strips on to the skewers like the rungs of a ladder; they can now be lifted as one unit. Repeat with the remaining chicken strips and 2 more skewers. Set these "chicken ladders" over the *parilla* (barbecue) and cook for 3–4 minutes on each side, until the chicken is firm and white inside.

To present Remove the skewers and let guests fill their tortillas with chicken, cilantro, and accompaniments of their choice. Squeeze a little lime juice over.

Roasted Corn

and Spiced Butter

Mexico taught me to appreciate corn—roasting or barbecuing it directly over the heat, still in its moistened husks, then sizzling it with spices makes this vegetable delectable.

Serves 8

Ingredients

3–4 garlic cloves, crushed

1/4 cup salted butter, softened

2 tsp. smoky paprika, Spanish-style

8 whole corn cobs in their husks

To prepare/cook Mix together the garlic, butter, and paprika and set aside. Pull back the husks of the corn and remove the silks; drip some cold water on each corn—about 1 tbsp. will be enough for each. Replace the husks and set the corn over a prepared barbecue, 2–3 in. from the embers or closer. Cook over the heat, turning them with tongs from time to time, for 10–20 minutes or until steamy and semitender. Now pull the dampened husks back completely to reveal the kernels. Replace the corn on the barbecue. As the kernels char and darken, add about 1 tsp. of spiced butter in little dots along the length of each cob. Let it melt and drip. Once the corn look charred in patches, remove them and add a share of the remaining spiced butter.

To present Hold by the husk and eat while still hot.

To eat
Iced black bean soup with chipotle cream *page 34*
Roasted corn and spiced butter
Chicken fajitas with salad
Watermelon and fresh lime
To drink
Margaritas *page 125* and/or iced beer
Vanilla coffee *page 120*

Beach barbecue

When you are lucky enough to have access to a beach and a portable grill or bonfire, you can really celebrate using this sophisticated summer menu. Shrimp, spicy harissa paste, goat cheese sizzling over potatoes, a green salad, all followed by ripe peaches flamboyantly cooked in cognac and triple sec, make for wonderful flavors in a beautiful setting.

To eat
Skewered shrimp with harissa
Potato and cheese salad *page 97*
Green salad *page 94*
Flambéed peaches
To drink
Chilled Chardonnay

Skewered Shrimp

with Harissa

Harissa and herb butter make these big shrimp on sticks very succulent and somewhat hot and spicy. If you cannot find raw shrimp use ready-cooked ones instead; reheat rather than cook, using the same spicy butter, but for a shorter time.

Serves 8

Ingredients

16 large shrimp in the shell (about 7 in. long)
1/4 cup harissa spice paste (see page 69)
1/2 cup garlic butter or parsley butter, softened (bought or made)
4 lemons, cut in half, to serve

To prepare/cook Holding each shrimp down flat on a cutting surface, use a sharp, serrated knife to cut the tail sections part-way through while leaving the head sections whole. The tail will divide into two, butterflying it. Discard the dark vein if you find it. Mash the harissa with the flavored butter. Use 1–2 tsp. per shrimp and coat the exposed tail surfaces of each. Thread the shrimp in twos or fours onto long metal skewers, looping them round to fit as necessary. Place the completed skewers over the glowing embers of the open fire, toward the cooler edge, or else rest them on a metal rack over the flames themselves. Once the shells turn rosy, brittle, and aromatic and the flesh, white and firm, they are cooked.

To present Present the skewers with the remaining harissa butter in small jars, for individual use, and pass each diner a lemon half. Have lots of paper or cloth napkins for messy, sticky fingers. Toss the shells on to the fire with the lemon skins to burn to cinders. They continue to smell delicious and it also avoids clearing up at the end.

Flambéed Peaches

with Cognac and Triple Sec

The color of this deliciously scented dish complements the other elements of this menu perfectly. Buy peaches that are fully ripe or buy them in advance and ripen them in a warm place.

Serves 8

Ingredients

16 small or 8 large ripe peaches
2 oranges
4–8 tbsp. clear honey
1 cup cognac, or more to taste
1 cup triple sec, or more to taste

To prepare/cook Halve the peaches by scoring around the circumference, twisting them, and removing the pits. Heat the peach halves in 2 large skillets over a corner of the fire (you may want to use old skillets for this as the flames may discolor them slightly). Tear or cut the oranges in half and squeeze the juice over the peaches; trickle the honey over. Add the orange halves to the pan, if you like, for extra flavor. When the peaches are warmed through and juicy, warm a large metal ladle and half fill with cognac, then top up with triple sec. Stir to mix. Hold the ladle near the heat and carefully ignite the contents with a long match or taper. Pour it, still flaming, over the peaches.

To present Spoon the peaches and their liquid into pretty dishes and eat immediately.

Clambake

This clambake menu is celebratory: lobsters, shellfish, and succulent steamed vegetables all cooked in an "earth oven" created by digging a pit in the sand, fire-heating stones, then closing the top. Trapped steam, inside, cooks the food.

Pit-cooked Lobsters, Shrimp, & Clams

(Clambake)

East Coast summer clambakes are an old idea. They can be done in a number of ways. The classic system is to dig a pit in the sand, line it with stones, and build an efficient fire in the pit. The food to be cooked is placed on a number of fine wire mesh "trays" which are then lowered on to the hot stones, often between layers of moistened seaweed, moistened leaves, or samphire. The biggest foods go in first. As steam works its way up over several hours, it cooks the food to perfection.

Serves 8

Ingredients

8 x 1 1/4 lb. live lobsters
damp seaweed, to cook
4 sweet potatoes, unpeeled
4 onions, unpeeled (optional)
2 x 1 1/4 lb. butternut squash, cut across into 2 in. slices
5 pints clams, scrubbed
5 pints fresh, live mussels, scrubbed
8 jumbo shrimp
salt and freshly ground black pepper
2 1/2 cups salted butter, melted or 2 1/2 cups extra-virgin olive oil, to serve
lemons (optional)

To prepare/cook First, get permission to build a fire if necessary. If possible, take a table to the site. Now dig a pit 1 yard by 2 1/2 ft. in area, and about 6–8 in. deep, in the sand. Line the base and sides of the pit with nonfracturing large stones. Make a fire with wooden kindling and charcoal in the pit and let it burn for 1–2 hours to heat the stones thoroughly. Have at least 2 pieces of fine wire mesh cut slightly longer than the size of the pit, with the ends rolled to make "handles" for lifting. Kill each live lobster humanely; hold it down carefully, and pierce through the head with a sharp, heavy knife. Scrub the lobsters briefly in a bucket of sea or spring water. When the stones are well heated and the fire has burned down, push the embers to one side. Place one wire mesh "tray" on the stones and cover with half the damp seaweed. Place the lobsters on top with the sweet potatoes, onions (if used) and squash. Add the second layer of wire mesh then the clams, mussels, and shrimp. Cover with the remaining seaweed and a double layer of foil to act as a lid. Put large clean stones on top to keep the heat in. Leave to cook for 2–3 hours or even longer. Uncover one side a little and test the food; it should be hot and cooked through.

To present Arrange the cooked food on several large platters, including the samphire which is edible, and let the diners help themselves. Eat. Enjoy the foods dipped into the seasonings, and then bowls of melted butter, or olive oil. Lemons are an option.

To eat
Parmesan and poppy seed "palm leaves" (palmiers) *page 18*
Pit-cooked lobsters, shrimp, and clams
Shredded romaine salad *page 96*
Angel food cake *page 106*
To drink
Chablis or Sauvignon blanc
Sun tea *page 119*

City barbecue

All over the world people have devised portable, earthenware grills and barbecues. In Tunisia and Greece, the ceramic barbecues are knee-high with a perforated grid inside for charcoal and an opening where ashes are removed.

Flowerpot Chicken

A friend, whose inner city garden has no space for a large grill, has devised a system to barbecue on his front steps: cooking food on a metal grill set over glowing charcoal, arranged on broken bricks inside a large earthenware flowerpot, This recipe is in his honor, but you can use any grill available.

Serves 8

Ingredients

8 small boneless chicken breast halves

1 tbsp. sweet chili sauce (Chinese type)

2 tbsp. virgin olive oil

2 tsp. finely shredded lemon zest

1 tbsp. freshly squeezed lemon juice

8 juniper berries, well crushed or chopped

To prepare/cook Pat the chicken dry. Make 2 shallow long cuts in the thickest parts of the chicken so it will cook evenly. Mix together the chili sauce, olive oil, lemon zest, lemon juice, and juniper berries. Rub this over the chicken in a shallow, nonreactive dish, turning the pieces in it to coat them. Prepare your grill. Set the chicken, skin-side down, and cook over a moderate heat for 6–8 minutes each side or until the chicken is firm, white, and the juices run clear or golden, not pink.

To present Serve hot with chargrilled vegetables and garlic toasts.

Chargrilled Vegetables & Garlic Toasts

In this recipe, the bread has a Mediterranean feel. Grill the bread over your grill or barbecue to accompany the chicken, either while the chicken is cooking or after its done. The chicken is delicious even lukewarm, but the bread and vegetables taste best hot.

Serves 8

Ingredients

8 garlic cloves, unpeeled and crushed

6 tbsp. extra-virgin olive oil

8 large portabello mushrooms

4 zucchini, halved lengthwise

1 eggplant, sliced widthwise into 1/2 in. rounds

2 small bunches cherry tomatoes on the vine

1 ciabatta, split lengthwise and cut widthwise into 8, or 1 focaccia, cut into 8 wedges

sea salt flakes and freshly ground black pepper

1 small handful fresh flatleaf parsley, to serve

To prepare/cook Peel 2 of the garlic cloves and mash up in the olive oil. Drizzle some of the garlic olive oil over both sides of the mushrooms, zucchini, eggplant, and over the tomatoes. Have the fire at a good even temperature but not too hot. Chargrill or barbecue the vegetables for 3–5 minutes each side until tender and aromatic, even if they look somewhat collapsed. Push them to one side of the barbecue. Cook the bread slices until lightly toasted. Rub and mash the 4 remaining crushed garlic cloves all over the toast to give it extra pungency. Drizzle the remaining garlic olive oil over the toast and sprinkle some of the parsley over.

To present Serve each piece of garlic toast with some of the vegetables; season with salt and pepper. Serve with the Flowerpot Chicken (see left) and the remaining parsley.

To eat
Green pea and prosciutto soup
page 32
Flowerpot chicken
Chargrilled vegetables and garlic
toasts
Fresh plums
To drink
Chilled Riesling
Elderflower tea *page 118*

Country barbecue

Baked Salmon & *Wasabi*

Effortless, easy salmon with no bones, skin, or debris, seasoned with *wasabi* and chili oil; faint Far Eastern touches which suit this occasion well since crab and ginger sandwiches also feature on this menu.

Serves 8

Ingredients

4$\frac{1}{2}$ lb. tail portion salmon, skinned and boned, prepared weight about 3 lb.

3 tbsp. chili oil

2 tbsp. ready mixed *wasabi* (green horseradish) paste

2 tsp. light soy sauce or fish sauce

2 cups baby spinach

To prepare/cook Pat the salmon dry on kitchen paper. Tear off a sheet of heavy duty foil; it should be more than twice the size of a salmon portion. Make a fold across halfway, so a salmon portion would sit comfortably in one half with a space all round. Paint or rub a tbsp. of the chili oil over the upper side of the foil. Set one fillet, boned side up, on one half of the oiled foil. Rub on half the *wasabi*, half the soy. Cover with the baby spinach. Paint or rub the remaining *wasabi* and soy over the boned surface of the second salmon fillet. Set this, coated side down, on top of the first fillet, to recreate the salmon's natural shape. Trickle the remaining chili oil all over the top. Fold the foil over to enclose the salmon and roll and crimp all the open edges to make a neat rectangular package. If traveling to another site for your barbecue, wrap the package in cool cloths. Once the barbecue is at the correct heat, not too strong, set the parcel above it and leave to cook for 12–20 minutes on each side, turning it over by the edges. Uncover carefully and check doneness; serve slightly underdone or according to taste.

To present Leave the salmon in its wraps; simply roll the foil back to reveal the fish. Let diners help themselves.

Why not prepare some stylish sandwiches, packed snug in their own sourdough loaf container; some rice salad; take some filleted salmon, asparagus, tomatoes, and two portable barbecues and head off for the country in two cars? On site willing helpers can cook the fish and the vegetables; others assemble the dessert. This is a wonderful menu for any occasion.

Chargrilled Asparagus with Fontina & Garlic Tomatoes

Ready-seasoned baby tomatoes and asparagus with melted cheese, hot from the grill, make a delicious accompaniment to open-air feasts.

Serves 8

Ingredients

2 generous bunches (about 2 lb.) plump green asparagus

2 small bunches of cherry or mini plum-type tomatoes, on the vine if possible

4 garlic cloves, cut into long slivers

extra-virgin olive oil (infused with basil if you like)

sea salt flakes and freshly ground black pepper

9 oz. fontina, Gruyère or Emmental cheese, in $\frac{1}{2}$ in. cubes

To prepare/cook Snap off any tough stems from the asparagus. Blanch it briefly in a large skillet of boiling water; drain and plunge into a bowl of iced water. Drain. Make a small hole near the top stem area of each tomato and push a sliver of garlic into each. Drizzle some olive oil over the asparagus and tomatoes to coat, and sprinkling with salt and pepper. Arrange the tomatoes and asparagus on a fine metal rack and barbecue until the tomatoes are wrinkled, hissing and sizzling; 3–4 minutes, turning the asparagus spears with tongs. Remove the tomatoes by the stems and snip each bunch into four. Roll the asparagus spears close together and sprinkle the cubed cheese on top. Part cover the asparagus with some foil or a pan lid until the cheese has melted.

To present Add another trickle of olive oil, and salt and pepper to the tomatoes, and serve the asparagus, with its runny cheese, straight from the barbecue. Eat both with your hands, taking care not to burn your mouth.

To eat

Crab and ginger sandwiches *page 44*

Baked salmon and *wasabi*

Chargrilled asparagus with fontina and garlic tomatoes

Wild rice salad *page 100*

Raspberry fool with meringues *page 113*

To drink

Chilled Sancerre

Armagnac and coffee

Backyard barbecue

Hot Beef Satays

with Herbs

These quick beef satays have a subtly sweet Asian savor. They take moments to prepare—a brief time to cook. Garnish them with fresh herbs at serving time, such as basil.

Serves 8

Ingredients

4 tbsp. canned coconut milk

2 tbsp. dark soy sauce

1 tbsp. dark soft brown sugar

4 in. fresh lemongrass, thinly sliced widthwise

4 red or green bird's eye chilies, sliced

2 tsp. freshly puréed garlic

2 tsp. grated fresh ginger

1 1/2 lb. rump or sirloin steak, in 1/2 in. cubes

1 handful basil, torn

To prepare/cook Soak 16 short satay sticks or bamboo or wood skewers in water while the satay ingredients are prepared. Mix together the first 7 ingredients to make the marinade. Thread equal amounts of beef cubes on the skewers. Set these on a shallow, nonreactive plate. Pour the marinade over. Turn the satays once and leave for at lest 5 minutes. Barbecue over glowing embers or chargrill for about 2 minutes each side, basting with the marinade, until golden outside but still slightly rosy inside.

To present Eat hot or cool, scattered with basil.

Variation

Substitute chicken breast for the steak, if you like, add 1/2 tsp. turmeric (optional) and use light soy sauce instead of dark.

Easy, backyard barbecues, in summer or autumn, including one or two simple, special additions needing no cooking whatsoever, can create a relaxed atmosphere. It helps if you can buy oysters already opened and ready to serve, and a have a great cheese store near you. The beef satays and skewered potatoes are all you need for a delicious outdoor meal.

Skewered Potatoes

An easy, tasty idea made simpler by having the baby new potatoes part-cooked before they are grilled. The crusty, crunchy outsides are really tempting. If you can, cook the new potatoes for this dish the day before the barbecue and refrigerate them.

Serves 8

Ingredients

4 1/2 lb. new baby potatoes, scrubbed

6 tbsp. salted butter, softened

2 tbsp. extra-virgin olive oil

2 tbsp. clear honey

4 scallions, finely chopped

sea salt flakes and roughly crushed black pepper

To prepare/cook Boil or steam the baby potatoes until barely cooked and still firm. Drain. Have at least 8 flat metal skewers ready. Push an equal number of potatoes on to each skewer. Mix together the butter, oil, honey, and half the scallions. Dab or brush this all over the skewered potatoes. Cook them, at a reasonable distance from the heat source, for 3–5 minutes each side or until golden and crusty. It may take a little longer.

To present Sprinkle the remaining scallions, the sea salt, and pepper on top, and serve.

To eat
Iced rock oysters with lemon
Hot beef satays with herbs
Skewered potatoes
Munster with pears *page 109*
To drink
Cabernet-Merlot
Armagnac and coffee

Marinades for grills

These spicy, aromatic mixtures, both dry and wet, can be used to give a lively, ethnic-style flavor boost to many basic grill recipes. Rub them in, sprinkle them over, use them as coatings, seasonings, and straight marinades. Even dry mix marinades, with olive oil and some added acidity (lemon juice, vinegar, wine) become flavorful tenderizers. And the wet mixes are invaluable as sauces or dressings in their own right.

Bombay Spice Mix

Old Bombay seems to me one of the world's most fascinating places, and the foods there made my palate rejoice. Its foods present a feast of colors, textures, spiciness, sweetness, and saltiness. Asafetida lends a curious pungent charm; it is optional but it integrates beautifully into the finished mix. It can be found in Indian markets.

Makes about 4^1/$_2$ oz.

Ingredients

2 cinnamon sticks, crushed

2 tbsp. coriander seeds

1 tbsp. fenugreek seeds

^{1}/$_2$ oz. dried crushed hot red chilies

1 tbsp. cloves

6–8 dried bay leaves, crumbled

^{1}/$_4$ cup coarse salt crystals

2 tsp. asafetida powder (optional)

1 tbsp. nigella or black cumin seeds

To prepare/cook Combine the first 6 ingredients in a heavy iron pan or wok. Dry roast until aromatic, then cool. Using a large mortar and pestle or an electric spice grinder, grind these to a powder, adding the salt toward the end. Stir in the asafetida powder (if using) and nigella seeds.

To present Present in a stoppered jar. Use in spicy Indian dishes as a coating, a seasoning, or a dry marinade.

"Ali Berbère" Mix

This dry spice mix, based upon one called Berbère, can be used to rub over meats, fish, or chicken before cooking. North African *tagines* contain similar sorts of spicy coatings to impart color, flavor, and tenderness. Use this dry mix to spice up your grills, chargrills, and roasts.

Makes about 4^1/$_2$ oz.

Ingredients

2 tbsp. dried black peppercorns

2 tbsp. allspice berries

1 tbsp. whole cloves

2 tbsp. dried hot red chilies

2 in. piece cinnamon, crumbled

1 tbsp. coriander seeds

1 nutmeg, grated

20 green cardamom pods, crushed

2 tsp. turmeric powder

2 tsp. dried ginger

To prepare/cook Put the peppercorns, allspice, cloves, chilies, cinnamon, and coriander into a dry skillet or wok. Heat briefly, stirring, until they begin to smell aromatic. Do not let them darken and scorch or they will be bitter. Tip them out of the pan and cool them. Add the grated nutmeg, cardamoms, turmeric, and ginger. Using a big mortar and pestle or an electric spice grinder, pound or grind the mixture to a coarse dry powder. Cool.

To present Store in jars and use at an alfresco meal as you like.

Mexican-style Mix

Color, intense flavors, and zest are all hallmarks of Mexican cooking. Spice mixes are created and passed on as precious gifts. In this mix, achiote powder provides a distinct flavor and gives a golden glow to the food.

Makes about 4 oz.

Ingredients

2 tbsp. allspice berries

1 tsp. dried oregano

2 tsp. achiote powder

^{1}/$_2$ oz. dried *chipotle* (smoked, dried jalapeño), torn into tiny pieces

4 tbsp. mild or hot paprika

4 tbsp. soft dark brown sugar

1 tbsp. coarse salt crystals or kosher salt

1 tsp. lemon pepper

To prepare/cook Combine the allspice, oregano, achiote powder, and *chipotle* in a dry pan and dry roast briefly over the heat. Do not let them scorch, merely become aromatic. Cool these. Put them, the paprika, half of the sugar, all of the salt, and the lemon pepper into a mortar and pestle or electric spice grinder, and pound or grind to a gritty powder. Stir in the remaining sugar.

To present Store in a stoppered bottle or screw-top jar. Use as required.

Note:

Achiote (or annatto) powder is found in Spanish and Latin American markets. If you cannot find it, you can use achiote seeds but you'll need an electric spice grinder to grind them really well. Begin by grinding them with the salt and paprika to give more bulk then dry roast the mixture with the allspice, oregano, and chipotle. Continue as instructed above.

Harissa

In North Africa, harissa is a popular hot, red, spicy, condiment. It is frequently served with couscous. Don't limit its use only to this, however; use it stirred into mayonnaise, soft cheese, or yogurt, or shake it up in vinaigrette. Use it, also, on its own, as a seasoning. Take a little jar along with you on your next picnic or portable feast.

Makes scant 2 cups

Ingredients

1 oz. large, dried hot red chilies, crumbled

1 carrot, sliced

2 large red bell peppers, cored, deseeded, cubed

8 garlic cloves, crushed

1 tsp. salt, or more to taste

2 tbsp. green cardamom pods to yield 1/2 tsp. black seeds

2 tbsp. each of cumin and coriander seeds

1 tbsp. black peppercorns

5 tbsp. extra-virgin olive oil

To prepare/cook Cover the chilies, carrot, and red bell peppers in a medium saucepan, with about 2 in. of boiling water. Bring pan contents back to boiling, cover, reduce to a lively simmer, and cook for 15 minutes or until tender. Drain the solids. Put them into a food processor. In a mortar and pestle, pound the garlic, salt, black cardamom seeds (having discarded the seed pods), the cumin and coriander seeds, and black peppercorns. Add to the food processor with 2/3 of the olive oil and process to a rough paste. Taste and add more salt if necessary. Spoon the harissa into one medium, or several small sterilized, jars, leaving 1/2 in. headroom. Pour on the remaining olive oil as a seal. Refrigerate, once cooled, for up to 1 month, topping up the olive oil seal after each use.

To present Present in the container.

Peri Peri Wet Mix

Part African, part Portuguese, this vinaigrette-type mix will enliven any meat, fish, chicken, or game you use it with. It is also good with pasta or couscous—it adds powerful heat, so use with care.

Makes about 2/3 cup

Ingredients

2 tbsp. dried, or 4 tbsp. fresh red bird's eye chilies, half crumbled or chopped, half left whole

4 garlic cloves, chopped

shredded zest and juice of 2 limes

7 tbsp. peanut or corn oil

1 tsp. sea salt flakes

To prepare/make Pierce the whole chilies with a pin. Shake up all the ingredients in a pretty, stoppered glass jar or flask, ideally with a nonmetal lid. Use as a marinade, to baste, or as a salad dressing.

Provençal Wet Mix

The foods you eat in Provence in France have some of the most intense flavors ever. Sun and ancient soils, no doubt contribute to it. I tasted a vinaigrette mix, very like this, one sunny Saturday. It's the lavender that is so haunting, and the hint of orange. But use it fresh to exploit the vivid tastes.

Makes about 2/3 cup

Ingredients

2 tsp. sea salt flakes

3 garlic cloves, crushed, but left whole

7 tbsp. extra-virgin olive oil

2 tbsp. red wine vinegar

2 stems (about 6 in. total) fresh rosemary, bruised

8 fresh heads lavender, crumbled (or 1/2 tsp., dried)

3 in. strip fresh orange zest, crushed

8 fresh basil leaves, torn or chopped

To prepare/make Pound the garlic and salt together using a mortar and pestle to make a paste. Combine this with the remaining ingredients in a large sealable glass jar or a flask with a cork stopper. Shake well. Leave in a warm place. Use within 1 day. Great for salads, for tenderizing red meats, and for use with roasted, cold chicken. Also for pouring over grilled goat cheese in a salad.

Picnic

Picnics rarely happen without a few bursts of delighted laughter. Appetites seem sharpened; food tastes better out of doors for some mysterious, inexplicable reason. Perhaps it's the sense of adventure, the spur of improvisation. Will the sunshine last? Can we keep the Riesling chilled? Consider, too, that picnics can happen in boardrooms, on train and bike rides. Picnicking can easily become a passion.

Bento picnic *page 74*

Orchard picnic *page 78*

Garden picnic *page 86*

Summer isn't really summer without a picnic. But picnics and portable feasts can be arranged for many different situations and in the blink of an eye. This is much of the reason for their charm. Spontaneity, a little bit of daring, can make the most simple picnic into a memorable one.

Portable food requires a bit of creativity and, at times, ingenuity. Invention often spells fun, so gaiety is often a natural outcome. Food tastes best when people feel relaxed so these ideas are ideal for enjoyable picnics.

Sand in the sandwiches, caterpillars in the salad: these can spoil the happiest of occasions, however, so some tips about organization are useful. Many are included here. On the other hand, iced soup sipped at the beach, or strawberries, cream, and meringues under the blossom trees can seem superb celebrations in themselves—really easy, simple ones.

Picnics are often successful because the young can run about, jump, play, hide, explore, and come back, exhausted and hungry, to dig into their food with their hands. Gourmet picnickers often use seasonal treats or regional specialties as a spur for their own feasts. Local breads, organically produced wines, unusual salad herbs, handmade goat cheeses, and pick-your-own berries or stone fruits can be the basis for wonderful, epicurean meals alfresco.

In other words, picnicking can be anything and all that you need it to be. Picnics often imply an element of surprise, of impromptu performance, even of risk. Rain might fall, the tablecloth may almost blow away; the Brie will be running out of its box, but boredom will certainly not be a problem. Huge appetites, laughter, and participation are much more likely. As long as some common sense has played its part and the food and drink are appropriate, not too ambitious nor too difficult to carry, or to eat; as long as wine glasses remain unbroken, some peppercorns stay in the pepper grinder, and the melon doesn't roll into the lake, there's a chance that the day will be a success.

My picnic ideas are traditional and also eclectic; elegant and also earthy; sometimes complex but more often very simple. A combination of homemade, store-bought, and communally provided items can easily add up to a splendid feast; trust your instincts and the weather, and enjoy.

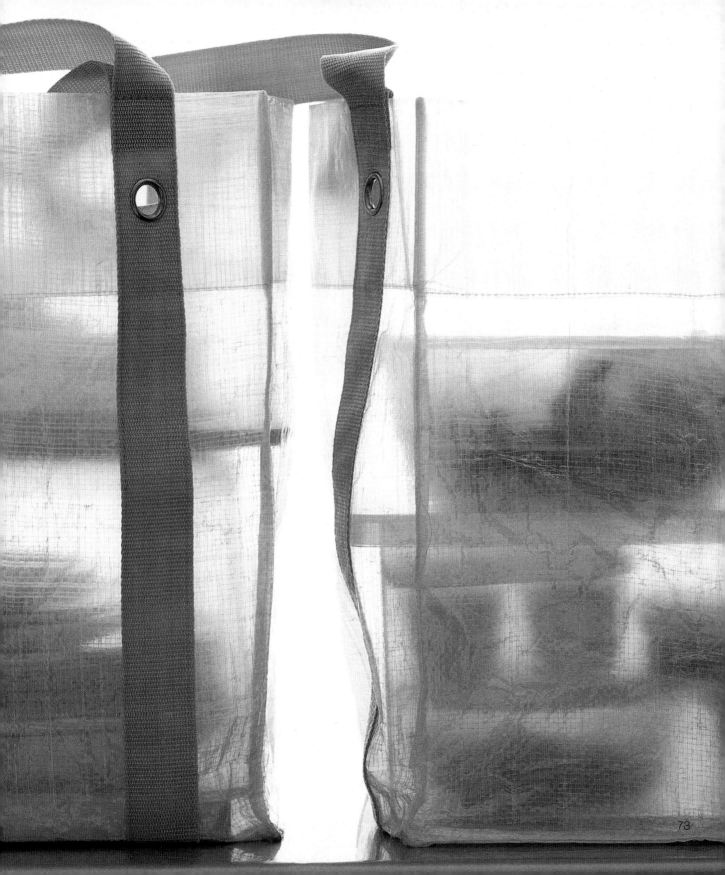

Sashimi of Salmon & Tuna

Always use sushi-grade, raw fish from a reputable source for this recipe. Alternatively substitute prepared smoked salmon in the piece, or cooked shrimp tails, if you prefer. Keep the fish very chilled. Pack it tightly into the box with no room for movement. Perilla leaves (also called *shiso* or Japanese basil), green or purple, have an intense flavor. Japanese stores often stock them, fresh, but nasturtium leaves are an alternative.

Serves 1

Ingredients

2 oz. sushi grade raw salmon

2 oz. raw belly tuna

4 fresh perilla leaves or nasturtium leaves (optional)

1 oz. shredded white daikon radish, to garnish (optional)

1 small packet/tube *wasabi* paste (green horseradish)

1 small packet/jar pickled pink ginger

1 small bottle or jar of *shoyu* sauce (soy sauce)

tropical fruits, e.g., lychees or mangos

To prepare/make Holding the fish carefully on a clean surface, skin-side uppermost, use a cleaver or sharp knife to cut it into 1/2 x 3/4 in. bite-sized pieces. Keep the fish in its original shape. If using the leaves, pack them into the appropriate section of the bento box or divided lunch box, or wrap them in waxed paper. Add the radish garnish either in its own section or else in waxed paper, as well. Pack the condiments, in their own containers, nearby.

To present Add the can or bottle of chilled green tea, wrapped in a cloth, and the washed, clean tropical fruits to the box. Seal well. Pack chopsticks and a china spoon. Secure it all tightly or tie well with its band, with ribbons or its ties.

Sticky Rice

Japanese sushi rice, stubby and plump, is correctly cooked after a brief soaking time, in very little extra liquid. Use Thai jasmine rice or even Arborio rice if you prefer—less authentic but perfectly acceptable—but allow a scant cup of water for these.

Serves 1

Ingredients

2/3 cup Japanese sushi rice

2/3 cup boiling water

1 tsp. finely sliced fresh ginger

1 tbsp. mirin (sweetened rice wine)

1 tbsp. white rice vinegar or white wine vinegar

1/4 tsp. salt (optional)

To prepare/cook Swish the rice around under running cold water until the water looks clear. Add more cold water. Leave for 30 minutes. Drain. In a medium saucepan, bring the rice and the measured volume of water back to a boil. Cover with a lid, reduce the heat, and cook for 15 minutes or until all the liquid is absorbed. Tip the rice out on to a plate. Leave uncovered for several minutes. Fan the rice to cool it and stir in the ginger, mirin, vinegar, and salt. Chill it if it is likely to become warm in transit since rice is a nonacid food which can spoil in warm conditions.

To present Pack the rice loosely into an appropriate compartment in the bento box or divided lunch box, separated from the fish and condiments.

Miso Soup

Traditionalists make fresh *dashi* stock from scratch using dried tuna and dried sea vegetables. It is delicious, very worth the effort, but if time is an issue substitute a good *dashi* mix from an Asian store.

Serves 1

Ingredients

3 oz. dried *soba* or *udon* noodles, boiled, or 6 oz. cooked, drained, chilled noodles

1 tsp. dark red miso paste

1 garlic clove, thinly sliced

scant 1 cup hot *dashi* stock (see above)

1 scallion, sliced into long, thin strips

1 sheet *nori* (dried seaweed), scissor-shredded, to serve

To prepare/cook Put the cooked noodles into a lidded bowl or appropriate container which fits well into the bento box or divided lunch box. Stir the miso and garlic into the *dashi*. Add the scallion. Pour this over the noodles. Cool. Chill in its container.

To present Pack the *nori* shreds, separately. Add the miso soup to the box just before it is secured.

Game plan for bento box or divided lunch box

Transport your box, cool, to your location. Uncover, unpack, and enjoy; dip the sashimi into *shoyu*, *wasabi*, and ginger, and eat.

Bento picnic

The elegance and deliciousness of the Japanese-style meal makes it the perfect picnic concept. Take this picnic from your office into the park, enjoy it as a theater supper, a celebration breakfast or brunch, or a backpacker's snack.

To eat
Sashimi of salmon and tuna
Sticky rice
Miso soup
Lychees and mangos
To drink
Green tea, spritzer, or beer

Park picnic

Garlic- & Anchovy-stuffed Roast Lamb

Leg of lamb is a prime cut and splendid as picnic fare. Cook it, ready-seasoned as in this recipe, with anchovy and garlic and it becomes a perfect portable feast. It tastes wonderful hot, warm or cold. The roasted onions which accompany it are also superb.

Serves 8

Ingredients

1 leg lamb, preferably spring lamb, about 5$1/2$–6 lb.

4 oz. canned anchovy fillets, drained and halved

10 garlic cloves, halved lengthwise

20 pistachio nuts, skinned and blanched

2 tbsp. extra-virgin olive oil

freshly ground salt and black pepper

4 red onions, unpeeled, halved widthwise

3 tbsp. aged balsamic vinegar

$1/2$ cup robust red wine

To prepare/cook Pat the lamb all over with paper towels to dry. Roll up an anchovy fillet half around each garlic half and each pistachio nut. Using a small sharp knife make a series of $3/4$ in. deep small cuts in the fleshiest parts of the lamb. Leaving the blade still in the cut, twist it, and insert the anchovy roll. Do this all over the upper part of the leg at intervals until it is studded with these aromatics. Place in a large roasting pan. Drizzle the olive oil all over the lamb and sprinkle with salt and pepper. Roast the lamb in an oven preheated to 375°F for 20 minutes per 1$1/4$ lb. and 20 minutes over: 2–2$1/4$ hours. Estimate roughly 45 minutes before the end of cooking time: add the onions, cut sides up, all around the roast. Take out the lamb when it is cooked and transfer it and the onions to a portable serving dish. Drizzle the balsamic vinegar over the onions. Leave the meat and its juices to "set." Now pour off excessive fat from the roasting pan and leave the "jus": stir in the wine. Cook, over moderate heat, stirring to dissolve the sediment until you have a rich thick red wine sauce. Pour it into a sealable container and pack it with the lamb and onions.

To present Carve the meat thickly on site, adding a share of onions, and the unthickened red wine sauce.

This picnic menu is a beauty: enjoy it under the trees, among the roses, or on lawns surrounded by statues. A Syrah would complement the leg of lamb, which is taken to the picnic whole and carved to order. Let scented Muscat flatter the cheese. Hummus flatbreads and salad leaves precede the feast, so revel!

To eat
Hummus *page 22* with flatbreads and salad leaves
Garlic- and anchovy-stuffed roast lamb
Muscat and *Banon* goat cheese
To drink
Syrah

Orchard picnic

A five-course picnic which could be fun to serve in an orchard or backyard. Serve the soup hot. Have the quiche, chicken, and salad ready and waiting. Let the pashka desserts be turned out on the spot if you like.

Portabello Mushroom Quiche

This earthy mushroom quiche is intensely flavorful. Do not be tempted to substitute button mushrooms: use big, dark portabellos. Sliced porcini would be the only other alternative; fresh or from the jar.

Serves 8

Ingredients

4 large, portabello mushrooms
1 tbsp. garlic and parsley butter (see page 39)
2 tbsp. extra-virgin olive oil
2/3 cup light cream
3 free range eggs, beaten
13 oz. short pastry, rolled 1/8 in. thick
1 slice stale bread, processed or grated into crumbs
small bunch of fresh chives, parsley, oregano, or a mixture, chopped

To prepare/cook Remove the stalks from the mushrooms; trim the stalks and slice them thinly. Wipe the mushrooms using a damp cloth but do not wash. Heat the flavored butter and the oil in a large, nonstick skillet. Add the mushrooms, gill-side downward, and the sliced stalks. Cook 5 minutes, uncovered. Turn them over, cook, covered, for another 5 minutes. Preheat the oven to 425°F. Using a fork lightly beat the cream and eggs.

Use the pastry to line a 10 in. fluted, loose-bottomed quiche pan, pressing it into the pan. Trim the edges and discard the trimmings. Halve each mushroom cap widthwise and put in the pastry case, gills up, in a decorative pattern; add the sliced stalks. Pour the egg mixture around the mushrooms. Stir the crumbs into the skillet to soak up any butter-oil mix. Scatter these over the quiche. Bake toward the top of the oven for about 20 minutes then reduce heat to 350°F. Cook for a further 15–20 minutes or until the egg is set firm.

To present Scatter the fresh herbs over the top. Serve in slices or wedges, hot, warm, or cool.

Italian-style Chicken Breasts

This easy recipe tastes good, transports well, and is perfect finger food. Because of the flavorful Italian ingredients it needs no seasoning whatsoever.

Serves 8

Ingredients

8 boneless, skinless chicken breast halves
5 oz. mozzarella, sliced into 16
4 oz. pecorino cheese, sliced into 16
8 sprigs rosemary or fresh basil, halved
16 slices garlicky salami, e.g., Milano
8 slices prosciutto
8 garlic cloves, crushed
4 tbsp. extra-virgin olive oil
fresh flatleaf parsley, to garnish

To prepare/cook Make two widthwise cuts, three-quarters of the way through each chicken breast half, at a slight angle. Push first a slice of mozzarella, then pecorino, then a herb sprig into each slash. Remove any skin from the salami, fold each slice in two, and push one into each cut as well. Continue until each cut is evenly filled and all ingredients are used up. Slide a prosciutto slice under each chicken breast half, and push a garlic clove between the prosciutto and chicken. Loosely wrap the prosciutto over the chicken. Set the prosciutto-wrapped chicken breast halves on a folded sheet of aluminum foil on an oven tray. Drizzle 1 1/2 tsp. of oil over each and fold the foil to enclose. Bake in an oven preheated to 400°F for 20–25 minutes or until cooked through. Refold the foil to enclose and wrap the chicken for transport.

To present Serve hot, warm, or cool, just as they are, removed from the foil.

79

Harvest picnic

Stuffed Quail

The only thing better on a picnic than a stuffed quail is a boneless stuffed quail. Look out for these in top-class game dealers, specialty butchers, and delis. Alternatively, opt for a variety of delicious cold meats such as salami.

Serves 4

Ingredients

8 prepared quail or boneless quail

1/2 cup seedless muscat raisins

8 slices prosciutto

1/2 cup toasted pine nuts

8–16 vine leaves, fresh, or preserved, blanched, and drained

1–2 tbsp. extra-virgin olive oil

6 tbsp. muscat-type wine (muscatel)

To prepare/cook Choose a large, shallow flameproof casserole or a metal baking pan into which the quail fit snugly. Mix the raisins, half the prosciutto, scissor-cut, and the pine nuts together. Push some of this stuffing loosely inside the cavity of each bird. Wrap a slice of prosciutto loosely around each bird. Set each wrapped bird inside a nest of vine leaves in the casserole or baking pan. Rub or dot each bird with a little oil or bacon fat. Splash the wine over. Bake the birds, uncovered, in an oven preheated at 350°F for 35–45 minutes or until rosy and golden, cooked through, and aromatic.

(Alternatively cook them hot and fast: 425°F for 20–25 minutes and serve them far more rare.)

To serve Wrap each bird for transporting, basting with the jus, first in foil then in a cloth. Serve hot, warm, or cool.

This stylish outdoor menu starts with radishes eaten with butter and salt, French style, and ends with Roquefort and grapes, the same way. In between, the offerings are more Italian: quails or salami, and saffron risotto—an unusual dish to enjoy at a picnic. A Côtes du Rhône would suit such food. Hot coffee and Calvados end the meal.

Saffron Risotto

Classic Milanese risotto uses Italian rice such as Arborio—a stubby, creamy grained rice which holds together. Buy it from a reputable deli or good supermarket. Although it's usual to add the stock slowly, stirring all the while, you can add it all at once, partially cover the risotto, and cook for 20–25 minutes, with an occasional stir. It's up to you.

Serves 4

Ingredients

71/2 cups chicken stock

1/4 tsp. powered saffron or 2 pinches saffron threads

6 tbsp. butter

4 tbsp. extra-virgin olive oil

1 onion, sliced

2 cups risotto rice

1 tsp. sea salt flakes

freshly ground black pepper

3 oz. parmesan cheese, in the piece

To prepare/cook Heat the stock in a large pan, and add the saffron, stirring it in well until it dissolves and gilds the stock. Heat half of the butter and all of the oil together in a large, heavy-based, skillet; add the onion and let it soften. Add the rice and stir until well-coated with the mixture. Add the stock, a ladleful (about 11/2 cups or so) at a time, stirring, and leave to cook gently until all the stock has been absorbed. Repeat this process about 4 more times over the 25–28 minutes it takes. (Alternatively add all the stock at once, stir, bring to bubbling, reduce heat to slow, simmer, covered, for 20–25 minutes, stirring now and then.) By the end it should be soft, soupy, but creamy. Add the reserved butter, and the salt and pepper. Spoon the risotto into a lidded casserole.

To present Take the parmesan in the piece. Serve the risotto from its dish—it's delicious hot, warm, or cool. Add curls of cheese to taste on site, using a vegetable peeler or sharp knife.

Romantic picnic

A romantic picnic for two should include indulgent foods, oyster, champagne, truffles. This menu follows the French tradition of serving oysters with spicy sausages, and includes a luxurious recipe for tagliatelle with truffles, all served with glasses of icy Champagne.

Iced Rock Oysters with Spicy Chipolatas

In France fresh oysters are often served followed by hot sausages; here is a version using spicy chipolatas. The idea is: pop an icy oyster into your mouth followed by a peppery hot sausage.

Serves 2

Ingredients

12 oz. skinless pork chipolata sausages or cocktail sausages

2 tbsp. cracked black pepper

1 tbsp. finely chopped garlic

3 kaffir lime leaves, scissor-cut

2 tbsp. soy sauce

1 tbsp. olive oil

12 fresh, live rock oysters

1 lemon or lime, halved

To prepare/cook Halve the chipolatas to make cocktail-size sausages. Mix together the pepper, garlic, and kaffir lime shreds. Roll the chipolatas in the soy sauce, and then in the garlic mix. Heat the olive oil in a nonstick skillet and cook the sausages for 5–6 minutes or until firm and golden brown all over. Pack in foil, then wrap in cloth to keep hot. Open the oysters and set them, deep shell downward in a container lined with crushed ice. Set the top shells back on the oysters. Pack a clean cloth on top to keep the oysters in position.

To present Unwrap and serve the oysters with the chipolatas, and lemon or lime for squeezing. Eat an oyster, then a spicy hot sausage.

Tagliatelle

with Truffle Butter

This tagliatelle has a touch of luxury. It is cooked in flavorful broth then dressed with some truffles. It can be eaten hot, warm, or cold—but do not chill. Truffles, black or white, are a seasonal delicacy; neither inexpensive nor easy to locate, though they are well worth searching for in specialty stores. Look for clean, dense truffles, aromatic and undamaged. Even a 1/2 oz. specimen would be sufficient for this dish. Alternatively use whole canned or bottled truffles.

Serves 2

Ingredients

7 oz. dried tagliatelle pasta

3 cups chicken or veal stock, heated to boiling

2 garlic cloves, crushed

salt and freshly ground black pepper

2 tbsp. extra-virgin olive oil

2 tbsp. butter

1/2–1 oz. fresh white or black truffle, finely shaved or shredded, or canned or bottled whole truffles, drained

2 squeezes lemon juice

fresh chives, finely or coarsely snipped

To prepare/cook Cook the pasta in the boiling stock until *al dente* (firm to the bite); drain. In the same hot pan, heat the garlic, salt and pepper with the oil, butter, and half the truffle. Add a squeeze of lemon. Put the cooked pasta into the pan and toss it carefully to coat. Transfer to a portable container and dot the remaining truffle over the pasta, scattering the chives on top, and adding another squeeze of lemon.

To eat
Iced rock oysters with spicy chipolatas
Tagliatelle with truffle butter
Arugula and parmesan salad *page 94*
Fresh raspberries
To drink
Chilled Champagne

Bicycle picnic

A bit of a surprise treat, this menu, with perfect lean fillet of beef in thick slices and old-fashioned baked potatoes: select a topping and add some herbs on site. Crisp apples, some dark chocolate, and Brazil nuts complete the menu.

To eat
Spicy roast beef
Baked potatoes with herbs
Apples, dark chocolate, and Brazil nuts
To drink
Beaujolais

Spicy Roast Beef

Cold roast beef fillet, rubbed with spices, and surrounded by its own juices. Great food for any occasion—any location.

Serves 8

Ingredients

2 1/4 lb. beef fillet, in one piece
2 tsp. allspice berries
1 tbsp. black peppercorns
1 tsp. cloves
1/2 tsp. ground mace
2 tsp. coarse salt crystals
2 garlic cloves, crushed to a paste
1 tbsp. vinaigrette
2 tbsp. extra-virgin olive oil

To prepare/cook Tie the beef fillet in 4 places, widthwise, with string so that it cooks in a good shape, pushing a metal skewer through it, lengthwise, for the same reason. Using a mortar and pestle, or an electric spice grinder, pound or grind the allspice, peppercorns, cloves, mace, and salt to a dryish powder. Mix the garlic paste and vinaigrette together. Place the beef in a metal roasting pan, and rub the garlic mixture over. Pat on the allspice mixture. Leave to stand 20 minutes or up to 1 hour at room temperature. Preheat the oven to 450°F. Heat the oil in a large nonstick skillet and brown the meat for about 8 minutes, turning to cook all over. Roast the beef for 26 minutes, no extra. If using a meat thermometer, the internal temperature must be 150°F for rare, 160°F for medium rare. The beef should be crusty outside, rosy inside. Leave the meat to stand in its roasting pan for at least 20 minutes to rest. Remove the metal skewer. If you must, refrigerate the beef, but it tastes better cool, not chilled.

To present Transport the beef whole or carved; serve in 1/2 in. slices, hot, warm, or cool, with any accompanying pan juices. (If cooked, cooled and refrigerated the day before, these juices may well have jellied.) Serve plain, or with some horseradish sauce and coarse-grain mustard.

Baked Potatoes with Herbs

Here's an idea for nicely portable baked potatoes; good for active adventurers to take on their journeys—classic but always sustaining and delicious. Add toppings according to what pleases you.

Serves 8

Ingredients

8 baking potatoes, washed and dried
1/2 cup garlic or herb butter
salt and freshly ground black pepper
handful fresh herbs, e.g., parsley, chives, basil, tarragon

Topping alternatives:
1 cup plain yogurt
or 1 cup grated cheddar cheese
or 1/2 cup sun-dried tomato paste
or 1/2 cup hummus or guacamole

To prepare/cook Push a long metal skewer through 4 potatoes; repeat with the other 4. Set them directly on to the top rack of an oven preheated to 425°F. Bake for 1 1/4–1 1/2 hours or until soft when pressed. Remove the potatoes from the oven and remove the skewers. Make a cross-shaped cut on the flat top of each hot potato. Squeeze slightly to open them, and insert about a tbsp. of garlic or herb butter; sprinkle with some salt and pepper. Press on the cuts to close them. Wrap each hot potato first in foil, then paper towels, then foil again. This way they'll stay hot for some hours, and undamaged. Take a selection of topping alternatives in sturdy jars with lids. Wrap the herbs in damp paper towels then foil and take along too.

To present Unwrap the potatoes. Squeeze open. Dot on some topping, add fresh herbs, and eat.

Garden picnic

This selection of charming, child-friendly recipes adds up to a good finger-food picnic for children of all ages. Homemade lemonade with soda and mildly carbonated ginger ale provide pleasant drink alternatives. There's also a do-it-yourself dessert.

Chicken & Parsley Salad

A simple, child-friendly salad which is plain and easy, yet surprisingly sophisticated for all its simplicity. A 2 1/4 lb. roast chicken easily provides 4 cups chicken strips.

Serves 6

Ingredients

4 cups cooked skinless, boneless chicken strips

2 tbsp. milk

4 tbsp. mayonnaise

2 tbsp. chopped parsley

salt and freshly ground white pepper

2 romaine lettuce hearts

about 6 sprigs watercress

To prepare Place the chicken in a portable container. Whisk together the milk, mayonnaise, parsley, and salt and pepper. Drizzle this over the chicken. Cover. Seal well. Pack the washed, still-wet lettuce hearts and bunch watercress separately.

To present Pull apart the lettuce. Lay the leaves in a neat row, parallel. Spoon a little chicken into each leaf. Snip or pinch off watercress leaves and sprinkle on top. Eat with your hands.

Tortilla Omelet

This is one of the world's most delicious and most portable of dishes but there are one or two authentic tricks to learn to make sure it emerges perfectly. If you want to cook individual tortilla omelets, sauté the vegetables in a large pan and cook the egg and vegetable mixture in small cast-iron skillets, about 5 in. in diameter—these will cook more quickly than a large tortilla.

Makes 6

Ingredients

7 tbsp. extra-virgin olive oil

4 medium potatoes, peeled, quartered, and thickly sliced

2 large Spanish onions, thickly sliced

2 red bell peppers, cored, deseeded, and diced

8 large fresh free-range eggs

1 tsp. salt

1/2 tsp. freshly ground black pepper

To prepare/cook Heat 4 tbsp. of the oil in a large heavy broiler-safe skillet about 12 in. in diameter and add the prepared potatoes, onion, and red peppers. Sauté over moderate heat for about 15 minutes, stirring occasionally. Cover the pan and cook for a further 15 minutes or until tender. Using a fork, lightly beat the eggs, salt, and pepper in a large bowl. Tip the potato mixture into the beaten eggs. Quickly wash and dry the skillet and return to the heat, adding the remaining olive oil. When the oil is hot, pour the egg and potato mixture into the skillet. Cook over high heat for 3–4 minutes, then reduce heat to moderate. Cook the tortilla omelet, undisturbed, for 10–12 minutes until the base is golden and firm. With a fork, pull back the edges of the omelet and allow the uncooked mixture to run underneath. Preheat the broiler and cook the top of the omelet for 2–3 minutes or until it sets firm.

To present Take the tortilla omelet in its pan, divide into wedges, and serve.

Salad & vegetable

Little seems more refreshing and welcome, in the course of a picnic or portable feast, than some simple, crisp, crunchy, salad leaves with a trickle of good dressing; a plateful of glorious greens. Some vividly ripe tomatoes or waxy baby potatoes can be utterly satisfying too. Such treats could comprise the bulk of the meal—especially if there's crusty bread, delicious cheese, and ripe fruit to follow.

Bacon, Arugula & Leek Salad *page 92*

Salad dressings *page 98*

Rice Noodle Salad *page 101*

Salads for portable feasts and picnics should be based on the fresh leafy salads, crisp vegetables, and fragrant herbs that are in season; on the grains, beans, root vegetables, pasta, and rice that are available; and on what can be bought en route. The ideal is vivid freshness, jewel colors, and clear, bright flavors.

Dressings are best made and packed separately and added at time of serving, although some salads improve with being dressed ahead of time, such as wild rice salads, bean salads, and pasta salads.

To keep salad greens fresh they need to be damp. Well-dampened paper towels will do; so will snap-top plastic boxes, plastic bags with a few ice cubes tucked into the base, and even a plastic salad-spinner, top, base and all, if you add a splash of iced water or a few ice cubes before leaving.

Some salad stuffs—endive, chicory, celery heads, whole cucumber, tomatoes, small romaine lettuces— can be washed and transported as they are to be torn or divided on the spot: participation is a good idea and fun for those unused to such activities. Don't forget a head of juicy garlic; it can bring a salad to life in seconds. Crush, chop, or rub it around the salad bowl or rub it generously all over a slice of French bread and toss this deep in among the salad. I like to drizzle some olive oil and salt onto my bread as well. Take oil bottles and pepper and salt grinders on every picnic and portable feast.

Dressings for salads can be as simple as you like: a scattering of herbs, crispy bacon bits or croutons, a drizzle of extra-virgin olive oil. Many of my recipes here include dressings. But if you take garlic, a lemon, oil, and seasonings, you ensure that any salad will have a dressing made to order.

Go for lovely oils; I'd suggest a bottle or stoppered jug of estate-bottled, first, cold-pressed extra-virgin olive oil as one of the most desirable. For Asian dishes, peanut, grapeseed, or safflower oils are good choices. Sesame oil, chili oil, truffle oil, hazelnut, pumpkin seed, or walnut oils are all welcome additions, but go easy, these become oppressive if overused. I usually mix them in the proportion of 4 parts of mild oil to 1 part flavored oil.

As for the acid factor, lemons, limes, or oranges, halved and squeezed on the spot, are a great bonus. Plain and flavored vinegars from fruit vinegars to wine or cider types can all add interest. Rice vinegars can also be appropriate. Balsamic vinegar is to be treasured, used sparingly for great effect (my rule is 1 part acid, 4 or 5 parts good olive oil).

Nuts and seeds add texture to a vinaigrette and mustard will help emulsify it. Salts and peppers come in many forms. I prefer flaky sea salt for its mellowness.

Pickled or dry salt-cured olives, green and black, can add appeal. Bell peppers, porcini mushrooms, and chilies can all boost a salad, especially one based on pasta, rice, beans, or couscous.

But remember: starchy foods and dressings should stay chilled to keep them safe for eating. Heat can cause spoilage. Take precautions to keep them cool, then relax and enjoy your alfresco meal.

Bacon, Arugula, & Leek Salad

Bacon, leeks, and fruit vinegar combine with arugula to make this superb salad.

Serves 4

Ingredients

2 medium leeks or 12 scallions

3 tbsp. extra-virgin olive oil

8 slices smoked bacon, chopped

2 tbsp. raspberry or other fruit vinegar

2 large handfuls fresh arugula

To prepare/cook Finely slice the white parts of the leek or scallions widthwise into rings. Put into a sieve or colander. Slice the green sections into 2 in. lengths, rinse well to clean them, then slice them lengthwise into slim julienne strips. Put these into a saucepan. Pour boiling water over the green leek or scallion shreds. Bring the pan contents back to a boil until the leeks turn a brilliant emerald green. Pour pan contents over the shredded white parts. Refresh leeks under cold water. Shake fairly dry. Pack into a salad bowl or a snap-top plastic box. Heat the olive oil in a skillet and cook the bacon until crisp. Remove it from the pan using a slotted spoon. Allow it to cool and wrap it in foil. Now pour the vinegar into the drippings left in the pan and stir to make a dressing. Pour this into a screw-top jar, flask, or bottle. Do not chill. Pack the damp arugula on top of the leek. Seal with plastic wrap if using a bowl, or close the lid of the box.

To present Toss the leek, bacon, and dressing with the arugula and serve.

Radicchio

with Red Onion Salad

This is a pretty celebration of colors, tastes, and textures.

Serves 4

Ingredients

2–3 heads radicchio

2 red onions, thinly sliced

1/2 cup raw baby fava beans (optional)

4 tbsp. extra-virgin olive oil

2 tbsp. hazelnut oil

2 garlic cloves, crushed

3 tbsp. balsamic vinegar

squeeze of lemon juice (optional)

1/2 cup salted, roast hazelnuts, coarsely chopped

sea salt flakes and freshly ground black pepper

To prepare/make Separate the washed radicchio heads but keep the cup shapes intact. Put the onions into a sieve. Pour some boiling water over them to blanch them then refresh immediately in cold water. Drain. Pack these in a salad bowl, snap-top box, or salad spinner. Wrap the fava beans in a twist of waxed paper and pack with the salad. Combine the oils, garlic, vinegar, lemon juice, nuts, and seasoning. Whisk or shake to blend. Take the dressing in a screw-top jar, flask, or stoppered bottle.

To present Using salad servers, toss all the components together with the dressing.

Arugula & Parmesan Salad

This salad takes seconds to prepare, and combines the lively taste of arugula with the robust flavor of the best parmesan.

Serves 4

Ingredients

12 oz. bunch of fresh arugula

about 1/2 cup high quality extra-virgin olive oil

9 oz. parmesan, preferably Parmigiano Reggiano

To prepare/make Take the arugula washed, not shaken dry, packed in plastic, a waxed paper bag, or a snap-top bowl. Pack along the olive oil in a small bottle or jar to the site. Pack the parmesan cheese and a vegetable peeler or sharp knife to cut it in curls or slivers.

To present When ready to eat, toss the arugula with the olive oil and add the curls of cheese last.

Green Salad

Always look for the freshest, crispest, and most flavorful lettuces. Take whole heads of washed salad and pull them apart at your picnic place. Pack herbs still in their bunches, washed, and cut or tear these at serving time. Take the vinaigrette (see page 98) or the dressing of your choice. Even a lemon, a little jar of extra-virgin olive oil, and some salt provide a dressing fit for a gourmet.

Serves 4

Ingredients

1 romaine heart, washed

1 Belgian endive, washed

2 handfuls peppery salad leaves such as watercress, arugula, endive, frisée, or ruby chard

1 small handful or bunch of fresh parsley, chives, mint, chervil, or tarragon

1 red onion, finely sliced

To make/present Pack the whole salad heads in a snap-top box or salad spinner, or wrap in damp paper towels and put into a big plastic bag. Wrap the wetted leaves, the herb bunch, and the sliced red onion, in its original form, in a similar bundle and seal. Take the dressing in a screw-top jar, or take the ingredients and combine them on site. Unwrap, tear, and combine the greens. Serve the green salad with your chosen dressing drizzled over.

Shredded Romaine Salad

This is a lively salad with a sweetish, protein-rich dressing.

Serves 8

Ingredients

2 heads romaine lettuce

Dressing:

2 tbsp. Dijon mustard

1 tbsp. honey

4 tbsp. plain yogurt

6 tbsp. extra-virgin olive oil

1/2 tsp. salt

2 tsp. poppy seeds

2 tbsp. cider, tarragon, or white wine vinegar

To make/prepare Wash the lettuce heads but don't shake them dry. Wrap in waxed paper or plastic, or pack in a snap-top salad bowl. Mix the 7 dressing ingredients, in brief bursts, in a blender. If it seems too thick, add a little iced water. Blend again. Pour into a stoppered bottle, flask, or screw-top jar. On site, pull off and pile up 8–10 of the outer, greener lettuce leaves from each lettuce. Roll them up. Cross-slice these leaves finely into shreds (this is called a *chiffonade*). Pull off the remaining inner, paler leaves. Leave these whole.

To present When ready to eat, shake the dressing, drizzle over the shreds of lettuce, and toss together. Arrange the whole leaves round the edge of the bowl.

Potato & Cheese Salad

Easy, versatile, delicious; this salad can be served warm or cold made using whichever potatoes you choose. Some lively green leaves are added, as an edible garnish, at serving time.

Serves 8

Ingredients

2 lb. smallish potatoes, scrubbed

salt

2 garlic cloves, crushed

1 1/2 cups cubed soft blue cheese

1/2 cup fromage frais

4 tbsp. extra-virgin olive oil

2 tbsp. tarragon vinegar

crushed black peppercorns (optional)

handful salad leaves, e.g. ruby chard, spinach, or frisée, to garnish

To prepare/make Place the potatoes in a pan and barely cover with boiling water; add salt to taste. Cook, covered, for 16–20 minutes or until tender but still firm. Drain them well. Turn off the heat and return them to the empty, dry pan. Cover the pan with a cloth and leave them for several minutes to dry out. Meanwhile make the dressing: put the garlic, blue cheese, fromage frais, oil, and vinegar into a blender or food processor. Blend or process to a creamy dressing, adding a splash of cold water if the consistency is too thick. Cut the cooled potatoes into halves or quarters. Pack them into a portable container or bowl; sprinkle with some pepper, if you like. Pour the dressing over the top and seal the container. Take the washed salad leaves separately in a sealed container.

To present Mix the dressing in well or leave it as a topping. Toss the salad leaves on top. Serve the salad warm, or cool but not chilled.

Salad dressings

Salads can exist without dressings but good dressings add undoubted allure. Sometimes the dressing itself tastes so good alone that it dominates the entire meal, *salsa verde* and mayonnaise, for example. Others, with an Asian feel, can add subtle freshness and charm. A classic vinaigrette, with its many variations, reigns as the most useful of recipes.

Vinaigrette

The classic recipe is one part acid to five parts oil. Vary this according to your own needs and the occasion, using aromatics, spices, and herbs as appropriate.

Makes about 1 cup

Ingredients

2 tsp. English or Dijon mustard

2 tbsp. wine vinegar or lemon juice

8–12 tbsp. extra-virgin olive oil

sea salt flakes and ground black pepper

To make Shake or whisk the ingredients together using a screw-top jar, a stoppered flask, a shaker, or a bowl.

Variations

Use grainy mustard. Add any of the following:

2 crushed garlic cloves;

crumbled dried chili;

1 tsp. clear honey;

chopped green herbs such as parsley, tarragon, chives, rosemary.

Mayonnaise

A classic but one which is made using a food processor; the texture is slightly more dense but this is lightened by the addition of boiling water. Take care when transporting this mayonnaise in warm weather and keep it well chilled.

Makes about 2 cups

Ingredients

1 egg, at room temperature

2 egg yolks, at room temperature

2 tsp. Dijon mustard

1 tbsp. wine vinegar

1/2 tsp. salt

1/4 tsp. freshly ground black pepper

scant 1 cup extra-virgin olive oil

scant 1 cup grapeseed oil

2 tbsp. boiling water

To make Combine the first 6 ingredients in a food processor. Process in a brief burst to mix. Mix the oils together and drizzle slowly in the oils with the motor running. Gradually increase the trickle to a slow, steady pour until the mayonnaise thickens to a dense emulsion. Stop the machine now and then to scrape down the mixture from the sides. Add the boiling water in a slow drizzle. Transfer the finished mayonnaise to an airtight container. Cool. Refrigerate for up to 1 week.

To present Spoon out into a bowl or portable container. Keep cool and use the same day. It tastes best eaten at room temperature.

Variation

Aioli

Add 4 crushed, chopped garlic cloves with the first 6 ingredients in the food processor before adding the oil.

Note:

As this mayonnaise contains raw egg, do not serve to young children, or to anyone who is sick, elderly, or pregnant.

Salsa Verde

A pungent, delicious, green sauce with an Italian touch. Combine the ingredients using a mortar and pestle, and pound together, or process briefly in a food processor in short bursts. Retain a chunky texture and clear color if possible. The crumbs are entirely optional.

Makes about 1 1/2 cups

Ingredients

2 oz. tiny pickled capers, drained

2 oz. canned or salted anchovies, chopped

2 oz. small pickled gherkins (cornichons), chopped

1 tbsp. gherkin pickling liquid

4 garlic cloves, crushed and chopped

2 tsp. pickled or dried green peppercorns, crushed

juice of 1 lemon (3 tbsp.)

1/2 tsp. finely shredded lemon zest (optional)

1 handful fresh basil, parsley, oregano, or marjoram, chopped

6–8 tbsp. extra-virgin olive oil

2 tbsp. fresh bread crumbs

To make Combine the first 6 ingredients in a mortar or food processor. Pound using a pestle, or process briefly in bursts to mash and amalgamate the ingredients. Add the remaining ingredients, stirring to mix. Refrigerate and serve within 2 days.

To present Serve at room temperature as a sauce for chicken, fish, broiled dishes etc.

Nuoc Cham

Light, sharp but aromatic, thin dipping sauces such as this are common in Vietnam and are becoming popular worldwide. They can be used to pour over or as a dip. Make this sauce ahead. Good with noodles, rice, spring rolls, rice paper wraps, broiled dishes, and leafy salads.

Makes 1/2 cup

Ingredients

4 tbsp. rice vinegar or fresh lime juice

2 tsp. honey or jaggery (palm sugar)

4 tbsp. chicken or vegetable stock

1 tsp. dark sesame oil, or more to taste

2 tbsp. fish sauce

1–2 fresh bird's eye chilies, sliced

1–2 tsp. toasted sesame seeds (optional)

To make Stir or shake together all the ingredients in a nonreactive bowl, screw-topped jar, or stoppered flask until the honey or sugar is fully dissolved. Refrigerate for up to 1 week.

To present Shake again; serve cool or chilled in tiny, individual dishes, or a bowl with a ladle.

Variations

Add 1 kaffir lime leaf, sliced in hair-like shreds.

Add 2 tbsp. chopped Vietnamese mint, garlic chives (Chinese chives) or Thai basil.

Omit the sesame seeds and substitute finely chopped, salted, roasted peanuts.

Wild Rice Salad

Dark, slim, wild rice (actually a type of wild aquatic grass seed) needs considerable cooking time; it has a nutty flavor and interesting texture. Cook it and dress it while it is hot; this way it absorbs all the flavors well.

Serves 3–4

Ingredients

1²/₃ cups wild rice, presoaked 2 hours if wished

3 cups boiling salted water

4 garlic cloves, crushed then chopped

¹/₂ cup virgin olive oil vinaigrette

1 bunch scallions, shredded

1 handful wild greens like corn salad, dandelion greens, or watercress

1 oz. fresh herbs, e.g., parsley, mint, basil, chives, chervil, or a mixture

To prepare/cook Drain the presoaked rice or rinse it briefly in cold water. Cover it with the measured boiling salted water. Bring back to a boil, reduce the heat, part-cover and cook for 45–55 minutes or according to the packet instructions. The grains should have "give" when pressed and some may have "butterflied" into a double-curve shape. Drain the cooked rice. Combine the garlic and the vinaigrette. Stir this well into the rice. Cool slightly. Pack into a snap-top bowl, or use a bowl and cover tightly with plastic wrap. Put the prepared scallions and salad greens of your choice, and the herbs into another snap-top bowl, or an airtight container such as a plastic bag. If using a bag, puff it up, full of air until it is tight, then secure with an elastic band; this keeps the greens crisp.

To present Toss everything together, leaving some of the herbs on top as garnish. Serve.

Variation

Add 4 hard-boiled eggs, shelled and halved lengthwise, to top this salad and make it into a full main dish, which can be served on its own. Follow it with crusty rolls, some superb raw fruit and some Brie or Camembert for a perfect, easy portable feast. Delicious!

Rice Noodle Salad

A fresh, flavorful salad with both Thai and Vietnamese influences. Add the separately cooked rare beef for avid omnivores and use fish sauce, but leave the salad free of meat, and use light soy sauce, for vegetarians; this salad works splendidly well both ways.

Serves 8

Ingredients

9 oz. dried wide rice noodles

1/2 cucumber, in julienne strips

1 mango, in 1/2 in. cubes or strips

2–3 bird's eye chilies, finely sliced

2 cups coarsely chopped fresh cilantro leaves

2 cups coarsely chopped fresh mint leaves

2 in. fresh ginger, shredded

4 tbsp. peanut oil

14 oz. cut of beef rump steak, at least 3/4 in. thick (optional)

4 garlic cloves, chopped or shredded

12 scallions or 1 red onion, sliced

1 tbsp. superfine sugar

2 tbsp. dark sesame oil

2 tbsp. fish sauce or light soy sauce

3–4 tbsp. rice vinegar

2 tbsp. toasted sesame seeds (optional)

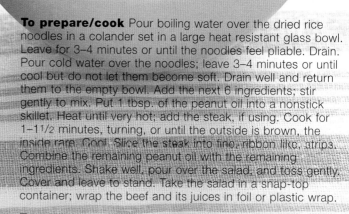

To prepare/cook Pour boiling water over the dried rice noodles in a colander set in a large heat resistant glass bowl. Leave for 3–4 minutes or until the noodles feel pliable. Drain. Pour cold water over the noodles; leave 3–4 minutes or until cool but do not let them become soft. Drain well and return them to the empty bowl. Add the next 6 ingredients; stir gently to mix. Put 1 tbsp. of the peanut oil into a nonstick skillet. Heat until very hot; add the steak, if using. Cook for 1–1 1/2 minutes, turning, or until the outside is brown, the inside rare. Cool. Slice the steak into fine, ribbon-like, strips. Combine the remaining peanut oil with the remaining ingredients. Shake well, pour over the salad, and toss gently. Cover and leave to stand. Take the salad in a snap-top container; wrap the beef and its juices in foil or plastic wrap.

To present Divide the salad between the serving bowls; add strips of rare beef for those who like it, adding some of the juices as well. Serve cool.

Sweet feasts

Ripe berries, candy from a local candy store, rich pastries from a favorite bakery, these are the simplest, most portable sweets to take on picnics and outdoor feasts. But included in this section are some interesting treats to try; cakes, cookies, some chocolate and fruit desserts, as well as the means to keep them looking and tasting good.

Pashka *page 106*

Mixed Fruit Salad *page 109*

Raspberry Fool *page 113*

Sweet things have probably been loved by mankind ever since wild honey was discovered, eons ago, and today most of us still regard one or two sweets as a must at the conclusion of a meal.

One classic dessert in Europe is cheese followed by fresh fruit and nuts. This is a good policy, especially if the fruit is scented and sweet, the cheese at its peak, the nuts mellow. But sometimes we want more frivolity; something small but sweet to intrigue our palates and make us feel indulged.

For portable feasting, ready-made cookies, cakes, chocolate, and set desserts, each in its own little container, are practical ideas.

Some dessert ideas can be made on the spot; crushing berries and sugar, folding them into cream, and crunching up meringues to add texture must be one of the most intriguing. This is included here, along with lemon-scented, chocolate-based, and nut-enriched sweet things.

Some have a rich dairy basis; pashka is an example, as is Munster cheese with ripe pears. Others are fruit based; my fruit salad is a wondrously eclectic one. Frothy white angel cake is a pleasure because it seems so summery and fresh. Yet it can be made in the depths of winter and served with coffee or tea.

Many of the other sections of this book will give you ideas for creating your own sweets. Pour some lemon cordial from the lemonade recipe (see page 122) over some thick plain yogurt or a bowlful of berries, add a crisp bought biscotti, amaretti, sponge finger, or nutty wafer and you've customized your very own dessert.

Many savory and sweet feasts can be concluded stylishly by serving a glass of some superb sweet wine or liqueur. The sky's the limit here but a small glass each will usually do nicely. There are great tastes to accompany coffees, teas, tisanes, the natural ending to many fine meals.

Angel Food Cake

with Citrus Frosting

Angel Food Cake, is made without any egg yolks so it is white, fluffy, and so ephemeral that it really does deserve its name. Vanilla, almond, and citrus flavors are a feature of this indulgent offering with its generous frosting.

Serves 8

Ingredients

Angel Food Cake:

7 egg whites, at room temperature

pinch of salt

1/2 tsp. cream of tartar

1 1/4 cups superfine sugar

3/4 cup cake flour, sifted

1 tsp. almond extract

Frosting:

2 cups cream cheese

3/4 cup powdered sugar, sifted

shredded zest of 2 limes and a little juice

1/4–1/2 tsp. almond extract

To prepare/cook Have ready a large, deep, ring-shaped cake tin with removable base (angel-cake tin). Do not grease or flour it. Combine the egg whites and salt with the cream of tartar, in a large clean bowl. Using an electric whisk or rotary beater, whisk continuously until the mix stands up in soft peaks. Set aside 1/4 cup superfine sugar; add the remaining superfine sugar, about a heaping tablespoon at a time, continuously whisking. Mix the reserved superfine sugar with the sifted flour. Fold half of this mixture into the whisked whites gently and firmly, using broad strokes in a "figure of eight" shape. Continue with the next half. Stir in the vanilla extract and smooth it gently through the cake batter. Smooth this batter into the cake tin. Bake at the center of an oven preheated to 375°F for 28–30 minutes. Reduce the heat to 275°F and continue to cook for 16–18 minutes. Test the cake; it should feel slightly springy to the touch and be shrinking a little from the edges. Remove from the oven and let it stand for 10 minutes; run a knife around the edges to help loosen the cake. Put a rack on top. Invert both quickly, giving a little tap to loosen the cake. Cool the cake on the rack. Beat the frosting ingredients together using a minimal amount of juice—it must not become too soft. Frost the cake all over and transport it in a snap-top plastic or metal cake box, setting the cake on the lid and closing it by pushing the base onto it from above. Keep the box this way up. Alternatively, cut the cake into slices and pack carefully in a transportable container.

To present Undo the box on the spot, when you are ready to eat, and decorate as you like.

Note:

If the day is very hot, try to keep the cake cool and fresh. Do not freeze it.

Pashka

with Fruits

Traditionally these little Russian desserts came as part of a spring celebration—a profusion of dairy products and dried fruits being some of the original features. But make them at any time, any season. Use one large bowl or several small "timbale" molds or even small glass tumblers. With the help of a strip of foil, each dessert is easily removed at serving time and the shapes stay perfect.

Serves 8

Ingredients

2 cups full-fat cream cheese

1 cup curd cheese, quark, or low-fat soft cheese

4 tbsp. citrus liqueur, e.g., Limoncello or Mandarine

6–8 tbsp. honey

1 1/2 cups fresh yellow cake crumbs

1/2 tsp. orange flower water

2 tsp. grated orange zest

1/2 cup chopped mixed peel

3/4 cup flaked almonds

To prepare/make Combine all the ingredients in a large bowl or a food processor. Stir energetically to mix or process, in brief bursts, in the food processor until the mix is uniform in consistency. Taste. Add extra honey if needed. Cut 8 strips of aluminum foil about 1 1/2 x 4 1/2 in. in size. Fold in half lengthwise, twice. Press the strips into 8 small, metal "timbale" molds (about scant 1/2 cup in volume) so the strips lie smoothly across the base and up the sides. Leave the excess to use as "handles." Spoon in the pashka mixture and press it down well. Chill for several hours or overnight. Transport to the site in the molds. Invert each dessert, and pull the foil strip downward, unmolding each one on to a plate.

Mixed Fruit Salad

with Passion Fruit

A luscious, fresh fruit dessert which is vividly scented and colorful. Substitute seasonal fruits for any of those suggested. What makes this special is the fresh passion fruit. If you cannot find any in your market, use raspberries or strawberries, or a mixture, but the flavor and fragrance will be different.

Serves 8

Ingredients

12 fresh passion fruit, washed and halved

1/2 tsp. orange flower, or rose water

2 tbsp. crème de cassis

5 medium fresh peaches, white- or yellow-fleshed, pitted and in chunks

4 fresh, ripe figs, green or black, halved lengthwise

4 ripe nectarines or red-fleshed plums, pitted and in chunks

1–1 1/2 cups cherries, still on the stalk

2 cups orange- or green-fleshed melon, seeded, in chunks

juice of 4 minneolas, tangelos, tangerines, or satsumas

To prepare/make Scoop the flesh out of half of the passion fruit. Combine the flesh in a blender with the flower water and the crème de cassis. Give 8 or 10 short, sharp bursts; you want to separate the seeds from the pulp to obtain an intense syrup. Strain the pulp through a nonmetal sieve and discard the seeds. Select a beautiful, but portable deep dish or glass jug. Add the syrup, the remaining passion fruit, halved but otherwise intact, the peaches, figs, nectarines, cherries, and the melon. Stir. Add the citrus juice. Stir gently.

To present Let people help themselves.

Munster

with Pears

Be brave; though unctuous and silky to eat and deceptively mild, the strong aroma of Munster is often enough to deter many a diner. It combines wonderfully with ripe pears.

Serves 8

Ingredients

small Munster cheese (a washed-rind cheese from Alsace), about 8 oz.

8 ripe but firm dessert pears

To prepare/make If your Munster is a little underripe, be bold; heat it, still paper-wrapped, in an oven preheated to 450°F for 5 minutes or else use a microwave (700–850 watts) on High for 2 minutes. This acts as an accelerated ripening process. The effect is intense. Take the cheese to the picnic just as it is. It will begin to trickle and run before too long. Leave the stalks on the pears. Using an apple corer, push upward from the base of each pear almost to the top stem area. Do not sever nor twist. At serving time, push down on the stem area and remove the core.

To present Unwrap the cheese just as you begin to eat. Leave the pears whole. Let guests use knives or fingers to eat their one hundred percent edible pear.

Pecan & Chocolate Brownies

Few people I know can resist a good chocolate brownie, soft, rich, and dark. Brownies combine well with all sorts of sauces, but are wonderfully portable when served plain or with a simple dusting of powdered sugar.

Makes 16 pieces

Ingredients

1/2 cup butter, cubed, softened

7 oz. plain, bitter chocolate (ideally 70% cocoa solids), broken

2/3 cup superfine sugar

2 eggs, beaten

1 tsp. vanilla extract

1 cup plain flour, sifted

1 1/4 cups pecan nut halves or pieces

powdered sugar, for dusting (optional)

To prepare/cook Melt the butter and half of the chocolate in a double boiler or heat resistant glass bowl over a saucepan of simmering water. Stir well. Add the sugar, eggs, and vanilla and whisk using an electric beater until evenly blended. Add the flour and use a spatula to gently fold it through the mix until it is a thick, rich, dark batter with no floury areas. Do not overmix. Prepare an 8 in. square baking pan by lining the bottom with parchment paper. Smooth the batter out into the prepared baking tin. Scatter the nuts and the remaining chocolate pieces over, pushing some well in. Bake in an oven preheated to 350°F for 17–18 minutes. The edges should look firm but the center barely cooked; the residual heat will continue cooking out of the oven. Allow to cool a little and score into 16 squares.

To present Transport in the baking tin, dusting with powdered sugar once cool.

Macadamia, Lime, & White Chocolate Cookies

Though these cookies need careful handing when newly cooked, crumbly, and still warm, they are easy and have a subtle flavor. Decorate them however you choose with the melted white chocolate. It may seem odd to use salted nuts, but it helps balance the sweetness of the dough and the richness of the chocolate.

Makes 24–32

Ingredients

11 oz. salted macadamia nuts

1 cup spreadable butter

generous 1/2 cup vanilla sugar

2 tsp. fresh lime zest, shredded

2 tbsp. freshly squeezed lime juice

2 3/4 cups self-rising flour

5 oz. white chocolate, broken

3 tbsp. light cream

To prepare/cook Toast the macadamia nuts in a preheated oven at 325–340°F for 15–20 minutes or so until they are dry, hot but not browned. Cool them. Hand chop 2 oz. of them coarsely and keep these aside. Using a cook's knife, mezzaluna, or a food processor in brief bursts, chop the remainder to a coarse meal, but do not over-process. Cream the butter and sugar using an electric whisk or rotary beater until pale and light. Stir in the nut "meal," the zest and juice, then the flour. Mix, then knead in the bowl to compact the dough into a dense, soft ball. Roll it out between two sheets of plastic wrap to about 1 in. thickness. Use cutters (hearts, diamonds, circles etc.) to cut out 24–32 shapes, each about 2–3 in. in diameter. Reroll any left-over dough and use this for more shapes. Lift the soft dough shapes using a narrow spatula and slide them off using a palette knife. Set them, about 3/4 in. apart, on 2 large baking trays lined with parchment paper or a nonstick silicone baking mat. Adjust oven temperature to 300°F and bake for 20–23 minutes or until pale golden, crisp but pliable. Remove the oven trays. Let them stand for 10 minutes then remove the cookies to wire racks to cool. Heat the white chocolate and cream in a double boiler until melted. Stir until smooth. Use a pastry brush to paint or drizzle the chocolate over the cookies or dip the cookies directly into the melted chocolate. Sprinkle on the remaining nuts, and press slightly into the chocolate while still warm. Cool until cold and set. Store in an airtight container, between layers of waxed paper, and serve and eat whenever you like.

Lemon Squares

This recipe is always a favorite. The sharpness and sweetness—the softness and crustiness—provide unusual but intriguing contrasts. The old fashioned charms of this sweet treat ensure its popularity.

Makes 16

Ingredients

Crust:

1 3/4 cups plain flour

scant 1 cup powdered sugar

3 tbsp. cornstarch

3/4 cup salted butter, chilled

Topping:

5 eggs, beaten

1 1/4 cups sugar

4 tbsp. plain flour

3 tsp. lemon zest, grated or shredded (from 2 lemons)

3/4 cup freshly squeezed lemon juice (from 3–4 lemons)

1/2 cup whole milk

1/8 tsp. salt

extra powdered sugar, for dusting (optional)

To prepare/cook Preheat the oven to 350°F and set a rack in the middle. Butter a 8 x 9 in. baking tray or jelly roll tin: it should have sides at least 3/4 in. deep. Double-line the baking tray with foil, overhanging at each end, and smooth it flat. To make the crust, put the flour, powdered sugar, cornstarch, and butter into a food processor. Process for 8 seconds then pulse minimally, in repeated bursts, until the butter is evenly distributed and the mix looks yellow and gritty in texture. Scatter this all over the foil. Press into the baking tray making it rise up slightly at the edges. Chill for 30 minutes. Bake for 25–28 minutes or until pale and golden. Reduce oven temperature to 340°F. Combine the 7 topping ingredients and whisk until blended. Pour on to the crust. Bake for 20 minutes or until the topping is soft and custard-like, but set. Remove and cool in the tray on a wire rack for at least 30 minutes. Use a pizza cutter or knife to mark into 16 cookies. Do not remove from the tray. Fold over the excess foil to cover. Wrap again in plastic wrap. Take the powdered sugar separately.

To present Pull up the foil to remove the cookies in one large block from their tin. Dust with powdered sugar if you like and serve. Use with tea and coffee, as a sweet snack, or light dessert.

Raspberry Fool

with Meringues

This is an ingenious recipe. The "impossible" meringue idea, from my sister Alison, works brilliantly and makes quick, foolproof meringues: 80–100 or so. These are small, crisp, and can be stored, in airtight jars, for months. But if you'd prefer to use purchased meringues, bought en route to the picnic, this too, is an option. The actual dessert is assembled pretty much on the spot: its crunch, softness, sweetness, and sharpness is a pleasant paradox.

Serves 8

Ingredients

"Impossible" meringues:

1 1/2 cups superfine sugar

2 egg whites

1 tsp. vanilla extract

1 tsp. malt vinegar

4 tbsp. boiling water

Note: Makes 80–100 tiny meringues. Substitution: 8 oz. store-bought meringues

Berry fool:

2 cups fresh raspberries

1 cup powdered sugar, plus extra for dusting

scant 2 cups heavy cream, whipped or 2 1/2 cups extra-thick, heavy cream

To prepare/cook Combine the 5 meringue ingredients, in order, in a heat resistant glass bowl standing in 1 in. of near-boiling water. Using an electric whisk or rotary beater, whisk continuously until the unpromising-looking mix forms a dense, glossy, stiff meringue which will keep its shape. Remove the bowl from the water. Set some wetted nonstick paper on 2 large oven trays. Wet the surface of these again. Put the meringue into a piping-bag with a 1/2 in. star nozzle. Pipe 80–100 small, neat meringues. Bake at 250–275°F for 1–1 1/4 hours or until crisp. Take as many as you want to the picnic along with the berries, sugar, and cream, in insulated containers. Take a bowl along to the site in which to mash everything together.

To present Mash the berries and sugar roughly with a fork and trickle this purée into the cream, adding whole or smashed meringues at will. Dust with a little powdered sugar and serve in glasses, cups, or platefuls.

Chocolate Cream Desserts

These are lush, luxurious, indulgent desserts to finish off a perfect meal.

Serves 8

Ingredients

2 tbsp. heavy cream

7 oz. dark chocolate, broken into bits

1/3 cup powdered sugar

2 tsp. ground cinnamon

4 tbsp. Amaretto di Saronno or Cointreau liqueur

1 3/4 cups mascarpone

1 box crisp crisp cookies, to serve

To prepare/cook Put the coffee or chocolate and chopped chocolate into a heat resistant glass bowl over a saucepan of simmering water and stir until melted. Sift the powdered sugar and cinnamon together and stir into the chocolate mixture, then stir in the liqueur. Mix until creamy. Fold in the mascarpone to obtain a marbled effect. Spoon, pipe, or smooth the chocolate cream into 8 small ramekins or jars to be taken to the picnic. Do not overfill them. Firm them up by placing them in the freezer for 20 minutes, or chill for several hours or overnight. Pack the individual containers into a larger box with a lid, or wrap them securely in foil into one large packet. Unwrap at serving time.

To present Put a little stack of crisp cookies beside each dessert.

Drinks

Tall, frosted tumblers, cubes of ice clinking, and the sounds of juice, water, or wine being poured into a glass—these are welcome additions to your picnic or portable feast. Sometimes a hot, sweet coffee, or a fruit-boosted smoothie are needed. Good drinks complement picnics in an uniquely satisfying way; try some of the ideas included here at your own portable feast.

Refreshing, appropriate, and imaginatively chosen drinks can enhance a meal in an enjoyable way. Even a well-selected bottle of mineral water can flatter the food; in fact most people would consider this an absolute essential. Some beer bottles in a wicker basket cooling in a mountain stream; a battered saucepan of aromatized tea or coffee set in the embers of a dying fire to heat—these are delightful, easy ideas.

But for the more usual occasions the obvious answer is to use insulated containers; vacuum flasks or jugs for hot or iced drinks, portable coolers which can be filled with ice; prefrozen "sleeves" to slip around your bottle of water, wine, juice, or cordial. Another idea is to create a special herb-decorated ice jacket around a bottle of frozen vodka and use this as a portable freezer in its own right.

Tea, coffee, and herb tisanes are easy drink solutions but elderflower tea, tea with rum, mint, or tea infused by the sun using just a jug of water are all included here. Quality tea, sold loose, is better than tea bags but this means you'll need a square of muslin and a piece of string to tie up the tea, or a metal, perforated, clip-closed tea infuser.

Vanilla coffee, an indulgent treat, is another idea. Serve it in tiny unbreakable cups, in mugs, or in toughened glasses or tumblers.

Many people who enjoyed their grandmother's recipes for lemonade, limeade, and ginger ale as children, have forgotten how to make them. I include recipes for these.

The cocktails included here are guaranteed to make any feast into a real celebration; from the classic martini (for grown-ups) to mint julep; from Silver Gin Fizz to Virgin Maria, a cocktail with no alcohol at all.

The joy is that cocktails and mixed drinks are so very diverse. They can be simple or complex; lemony or nutty; layered or blended; mild or potent; floral or herbal; decorative or plain; alcohol-boosted or absolutely alcohol-free.

For cocktails, you'll need a jug and shaker, or both, the glasses, a corkscrew, a bottle opener, a small sharp knife, a long-handled spoon, a drinks strainer which ideally fits over a pouring lip, a citrus squeezer (the wand type is useful), lots of ice, and the cocktail raw materials, ideally chilled. A "measure" is usually made of metal and holds 1 fl. oz. volume. Use a small shot glass as an alternative, or 2 level measuring tablespoons which is slightly larger but conveniently approximate. Otherwise take along a small unbreakable glass measuring jug.

Almost any appropriately sized glass will do, especially if it is made of unbreakable glass. Don't forget that waxed paper cups, plastic tumblers; porcelain, metal and even bamboo containers can all be useful and appealing as drinks containers.

Remember to offer lots of still and sparkling water for all who want it; in the end this is the most magnificent drink of all.

Frozen vodka

To make this decorative ice jacket, take a large empty plastic bottle and cut off the top just below the shoulders. Place the vodka bottle centrally in the plastic sleeve, and fill the cylinder with water. Push bay sprigs, pretty leaves or flowers, colorful berries, or lemon slices into the water around the vodka bottle and place the whole—upright—in a freezer for at least 24 hours. Take it to your picnic complete. The outer plastic will slide off when slightly warmed—either after the traveling time, or after a little warm hand pressure. The vodka will pour thickly. Enjoy its opulent cold texture and taste!

117

Elderflower Tea

These days, ready-made elderflower syrup is available at many specialty and gourmet markets. Though sweet, it is flowery and fresh. Use it along with a delicate China tea and, if real elderflower is blooming, add some washed heads of flowers too. If elderflower syrup is hard to find, use apple juice concentrate for a refreshing alternative.

Serves 8

Ingredients

4 cups boiling water

1/4 oz. China tea, e.g. jasmine

2 tbsp. elderflower syrup or cordial, or apple juice concentrate

2 fresh elderflower heads, if in season (optional)

To prepare/make Use a heat-resistant glass jug, vacuum flask, whatever pleases you and suits the occasion. Pour the water over the tea, tied up in muslin or in a tea infuser, and leave to infuse for 5 minutes. Remove the tea "bag" or infuser and pour in the syrup or cordial.

To present Push the flowerheads (rinsed in spring water) into the tea at serving time, if using. Serve in small cups, goblets, or tumblers.

Note:

If made double strength (using only 2 cups of boiling water) and poured over 2 cups of ice cubes, this can become a chilled drink, instead of a hot one.

Scented Tea

with Rum

Tea made with added aromatics can be very alluring. Select either China, Indian, or another exotic tea. Vary the additions according to the type of tea you are using.

Serves 4–6

Ingredients

4 cups boiling water

1 cinnamon stick, crushed

4 cloves

6 green cardamom pods, crushed

3 in. strip of orange zest or 1 in. piece of fresh ginger, bruised

1/2 oz. tea leaves

2/3 cup dark rum

1 orange, pith removed, sliced into rounds

To prepare/make Pour the boiling water over the cinnamon, cloves, cardamom pods, bring back to the boil, cover, reduce heat to simmering. Simmer for 3–4 minutes. Put the zest and tea, in a piece of muslin with a string attached, or in a tea infuser, into a vacuum flask. Pour in the boiling spiced liquid, including all spices. Stopper the flask. Infuse for 5 minutes then remove the tea and zest. If taking to a picnic, take along another flask of plain boiling water, and the rum in a separate bottle.

To present Pour the tea, and add slices of orange and a dash of rum to each serving of the hot spiced tea.

Mint Tea

Tunisian tea houses taught me how refreshing this hot, sweet tea can be. Don't stint on the fresh mint; it is crucial to its success.

Serves 8

Ingredients

4 cups boiling water

1/2 oz. green (unfermented) tea

5 oz. bunch (about 3 cups) fresh mint, ideally spearmint, lower stems discarded

16–24 sugar cubes or 8 tbsp. superfine sugar

sliced lemon or lime, to decorate

To prepare/make Pour the boiling water over the tea, tied up in muslin or in a tea infuser, in a jug or vacuum flask, adding half of the mint. Crush and press the mint then seal and leave to infuse.

To present Add sugar to each cup, glass or goblet, and a share of the remaining mint. Crush the mint and pour the hot tea over. Decorate with sliced lemon or lime.

Sun Tea

At its most homey, this can be made in a jug of water, sitting in a sunny spot with some fragrant tea bags suspended in it. Once infused, the tea bags are removed. This is the basis of sun tea. Boost it with a little lemon cordial, some sliced lemon, lime, or orange. Add a few sprigs of fresh mint, lovage, or bergamot. Ice and a top-up of sparkling water, ginger ale, or tonic improves it too. This is a thirst-quencher, alcohol-free, of simplicity and merit, and one often loved by the young.

Serves 8

Ingredients

6 good quality tea bags or 1/2 oz. loose tea (tied in muslin or in a tea infuser) e.g., China or Indian, mixed red fruits or Japanese green tea

4 cups spring water, tap water or filtered water, at room temperature

ice cubes

handful of fresh mint, lovage, bergamot, or lemon balm leaves

2–3 tbsp. lemonade, undiluted (see page 122)

1 lemon, 2 limes, or 1 orange, sliced

iced sparkling water, ginger ale, tonic, or even lemonade, to top up

To prepare/make Leave the tea to infuse in the nonchilled water. This may take 30 minutes or 2 hours depending on the temperature, the type of tea, and the situation. Stir occasionally. Strain. Pour into a flask, bottle, or jar. Take along the remaining items: ice, fresh herbs, lemonade, citrus fruits, and the top-up liquid of your choice.

To present On site, crush the herbs and sliced citrus fruit in a big glass jug with the ice. Pour the sun tea over.

Coffee

with Calvados

"Calva" with or in coffee is a delightful French idea. Add sugar—or not—to this fragrant coffee, depending on your taste buds.

Serves 8

Ingredients

2 1/2 cups freshly made, hot coffee

8 sugar lumps (optional)

1/2 cup Calvados, apple brandy, or apple jack

To make/present Transport the hot coffee in a vacuum jug or flask. Combine a share of hot coffee, some sugar, if liked, and some of Calvados in each coffee cup. Stir, sip and enjoy. Alternatively, serve the coffee as is, taking along 8 tiny shot glasses. Serve a shot of Calvados per person in each glass, as an additional pleasure.

Vanilla Coffee

In Mexico, Café de Olla, an after-dinner drink, is sometimes served in big, earthenware pitchers. Adapt this idea for your own celebrations. It is both festive and fun.

Serves 8

Ingredients

4 vanilla pods, sliced almost into halves, lengthwise

4 cups boiling water

4 tsp. cloves, bruised

4 tsp. allspice berries

1 1/3 cups dark brown sugar

2 in. strip orange zest, bruised

8 cups freshly made *cafétière* coffee, e.g., Brazilian

To prepare/make Scrape out the seeds from the vanilla pods. In a saucepan, heat together the water, vanilla seeds, cloves, allspice, and brown sugar for 5 minutes, stirring. Add the orange zest, crushing it down well. Turn off the heat. Let it infuse 2 minutes. Remove the orange zest, and take this spicy syrup, in a stoppered, heat-resistant metal vacuum flask, or in a heat-resistant jug which can be set directly on the grill, to the barbecue.

To present Reheat the syrup over the fire if necessary. Pour out some hot coffee into cups, mugs, or glasses. Add a top-up of hot syrup.

Note:

You could add half a cinnamon stick per person, too, if you like.

Smoothies, Crushes, & Variations

Although these can now often be purchased, ready-made, in supermarkets or made while you wait at a juice bar, your own customized combinations are freshest and best. Vary these according to the fruits available. To simplify the process use a half-cup measure or even a wine glass as your volume measure (about 4 1/2 fl. oz. or so). Keep the units constant. But relax, this is a free and easy concept. You'll also need a large and sturdy blender which is not damaged by ice. If using a juicer, juice the solids and use a blender to combine these with the rest if banana is used, or whisk or shake until cold and blended.

Each drink serves 4

Pineapple-Honey-Citrus Smoothie

Ingredients

2 parts natural yogurt, ideally with live cultures

2 parts cubed fresh pineapple

2 parts freshly squeezed orange or grapefruit juice

1/2 part honey

1 part ice cubes

To prepare/make Combine the first 4 ingredients in a blender. Blend. Add the ice and blend again until the ice is no longer visible and the drink is a thickish liquid. Add a little water if liked, to thin it slightly.

To present If made ahead, store it in a vacuum flask but take extra ice and shake the smoothie well to chill it again before serving, or pour it over the ice in the unbreakable glasses or containers. Serve with thick drinking straws.

Variations

Raspberry-Pineapple Smoothie

To prepare/make Make as before adding 2 parts fresh or thawed raspberries and use orange, not grapefruit juice. Blend these first 5 ingredients and then the ice cubes.

Plum, Banana, & Blackberry Smoothie

2 parts plain yogurt, ideally with live cultures

1 part fresh or thawed blackberries

1 part cubed, red-fleshed plums

1 part chopped banana

2 parts freshly squeezed blood orange or orange juice

1/2 part honey

1 part ice cubes

To prepare/make Make as before, blending the first 6 ingredients, then the ice cubes.

Mango, Raspberry, & Orange Crush

2 parts cubed fresh mango

1 part chopped banana

1/4 part fresh or thawed raspberries

2 parts freshly squeezed orange juice

1 part ice cubes

To prepare/make Make as before, blending the first 4 ingredients, then the ice cubes.

Home-Made
Ginger Ale

A favorite in England, this drink is rarely found these days. This recipe is easy and makes a refreshing drink. Use plastic, not glass bottles. Go for screw-tops. You'll need a large, clean plastic bucket and eight 1 quart plastic bottles.

Makes 2 gallons

Ingredients

2 tsp. dried yeast granules

3 cups sugar

2 tbsp. ground ginger

1 tbsp. lemonade, undiluted (see right) or 1/2 tsp. lemon oil

2 cups freshly squeezed lemon juice (about 8 lemons)

4 cups hot water

101/2 pints cold water

To serve: Ice, sliced lemon; drinking straws (optional)

To make Stir the yeast granules with about 1/4 cup of warm water and 2 tsp. of the sugar. Put the remaining sugar, the ginger, lemonade or lemon oil, and lemon juice into a clean plastic bucket. Stir in the hot water until the sugar is dissolved. Add the cold water. Stir in the yeast mix, with a whisk, until it is evenly distributed. Using a funnel, pour the ginger ale into 8 clean, flexible plastic bottles. Pour boiling water over the screw tops, and drain them. Pinch the shoulders at the top of the bottle to allow space for expansion then screw on the tops. Leave the bottles at normal room temperature for at least 4–6 days. During this time the pressure will increase; to start with the bottles have give; later tightness means that fizz and pressure are developing. If necessary, release the tops at intervals. Test one bottle; when the ale tastes slightly fizzy, refrigerate them all.

To present Drink chilled. Try to avoid shaking the bottles. Serve over ice with lemon and drinking straws.

Home-Made
Lemonade & Soda

My lemon cordial is brilliantly easy; use it with sparkling water, beer, in cocktails, in sun tea, over sorbets and ices, as well as with plain water.

Makes 3 cups (undiluted)

Ingredients

scant 1 cup water

1 cup sugar

zest, in fine shreds, and juice of 7–8 lemons (about 2 cups juice)

zest of 1 orange, in fine shreds

61/2 pints sparkling water, to dilute

ice, to serve

drinking straws (optional)

To make Boil the water with the sugar to make a hot syrup. Add the lemon juice and stir well; bring back to a boil. Add the lemon and orange zests, stir well, and remove from the heat. Allow to stand for 2 minutes. Strain well to remove the zest shreds. The color should be a bright golden yellow. Cool the syrup over ice. Pour it into a bottle, a vacuum flask, or stoppered jug. Keep refrigerated.

To present Take iced sparkling water, spring water, or soda to dilute it. Take, too, some ice cubes in an insulated container or buy some en route. Dilute about 1 part cordial to 3–4 parts sparkling water and serve with some ice cubes, and straws if you like.

Note:

Fresh herbs such as lovage, fresh mint, lemon balm, or even crushed kaffir lime leaves may also be added as a decoration. So can slices or wedges of any citrus fruit of of your choice.

Home-Made
Limeade

This recipe uses a similar concept to the Lemonade; adding extra lime zest boosts flavors. Add bitters or a little alcohol, if you like.

Serves 4

Ingredients

5 fresh limes, one with zest removed in 4 long strips

4 tbsp. superfine sugar

iced soda water, to top up

ice cubes or crushed ice, to top up

To make "Muddle" or mash up one strip of lime in each of the bases of 4 tall glasses with its share of sugar. Squeeze all the limes. Divide this juice between the glasses. Stir them again until the sugar is dissolved. Heap in some ice; half-fill each glass. Top up with soda water. Stir. Serve with drinking straws.

Variations

Bitter Limeade Shake in some Peychaud, Angostura, or orange bitters. Stir.

Chili Limeade In India this is sometimes called *nimbu pani*. Omit the sugar. Add a whole fresh chili to each glass, pushed on to a satay or cocktail stick, and a sprinkle of salt in place of the sugar.

Kaffir Limeade Add 1 fresh kaffir lime leaf (washed and crushed) to each drink at the end of mixing. Stir. (Substitute lemon-scented verbena as an alternative.)

Virgin Maria

This is a Bloody Mary without alcohol but with one or two other interesting ingredients and lots of ice to make it more refreshing. Give it either an Asian or a Mexican twist according to your mood.

Serves 4

Ingredients

2 fresh limes

2 fresh lemons

2 1/2 cups tomato juice, "clamato" juice or mixed tomato-vegetable juice

4 tsp. Worcestershire sauce

2 tsp. *wasabi* paste or 1/2 tsp. smoked hot paprika

2 tsp. light soy sauce or 1 tsp. sea salt

16 ice cubes

4 sticks fresh celery with leaves

To make/present

Remove long loopy curls of zest from the limes and lemons, and reserve. Squeeze the limes and lemons. Combine the tomato juice, lime and lemon juice, Worcestershire sauce, *wasabi* or paprika, and soy sauce or salt in a blender, shaker, or jug. On site, blend, shake, or stir. Pour into 4 portable glasses, preferably tall. Add ice cubes to each glass, a stick of celery to stir, and curls of zest.

Silver Gin Fizz

This is a shaken cocktail topped up with soda. Either mix the ingredients in a large shaker, add ice at the last minute, and shake, or else take all the ingredients separately and make the drink on site. If carried in a shaker, make sure it is chilled as it contains fresh egg whites.

Serves 8

Ingredients

16 ice cubes

2 tbsp. sugar syrup or 2 tbsp. superfine sugar

scant 1 cup freshly squeezed lemon juice

2 1/2 cups dry gin

4 fresh egg whites

chilled soda water, to top up

To make/present

Combine the first 5 ingredients in a large shaker or a screw-top jar. Shake until frothy. Strain into 8 lowball glasses or short tumblers. Top up with chilled soda and serve.

Variations

Outback Replace the fresh lemon with 2/3 cup of dry French vermouth.

Morning Glory Fizz This has 1 tsp. of Pernod added and the top-up is ginger ale, not soda.

Note:

For sugar syrup, boil 1 cup water and 1 1/4 cups superfine sugar until the sugar dissolves.

Mint Julep

For this recipe you need sugar, ice, bourbon, and good, fresh mint in decent quantities. To "muddle" two ingredients means to gently mash and crush them using a long-handled spoon to extract the maximum flavor and aroma. Any long-handled, blunt implement will do, even a knife handle.

Serves 4

Ingredients

about 16 large, fresh mint sprigs

4 tsp. superfine sugar

1 1/4 cups crushed ice

1 1/4 cups bourbon

To make/prepare Make these directly in the 4 long glasses or 4 silver mugs. Put 3 sprigs of mint into the base of each glass. Add the sugar. "Muddle" or mash these two well together to extract the flavors. Stir in some crushed ice into each glass. "Muddle" again. Pour in the bourbon. Stir. Top up with extra crushed ice. Add the remaining mint sprig to the glasses and serve.

Variations

Mint-Lime Julep Add a thick wedge of lime to the mint-sugar mix. Continue as above.

Bitter Mint-Lime Julep To either of the drinks mentioned above add 2 shakes of Peychaud's or Angostura bitters to each glass. Do not stir. Leave as a "blush." Drink through drinking straws.

Pisco Julep Substitute Pisco (Peruvian grape brandy) for the bourbon.

Applejack Julep Use applejack, Calvados, or apple brandy in place of the bourbon.

Grown-up Martini

Some grown-up drinkers, serious martini *aficionados*, merely pass the vermouth bottle, still closed, over the top of the glass adding not a drop. This requires real dedication. Others rinse out the glass with it—a bit of a waste in my view. Here is a fairly standard recipe, rather stronger than usual, which is stirred, not shaken.

Serves 8

Ingredients

1 1/2 cups London dry gin

4 tbsp. dry vermouth

12–16 ice cubes

8 green olives (optional)

8 x 3 in. strips of lemon zest (optional)

To make Have the 8 glasses ready chilled; put them in the freezer for at least an hour or pack in an insulated bag full of ice for outdoor feasts. Stir the gin and the vermouth together in a large jug over the ice cubes. Into each glass pour a share of the martini. Drop in an olive or a lemon twist. Alternatively twist the lemon above each drink or rub the zest around the glass rim.

Variations

Gin & It Substitute dry red vermouth for the dry vermouth, but use equal quantities of gin and vermouth.

Vodkatini Substitute Russian-type vodka for the gin. Reduce the dry vermouth to 2 1/2–3 tbsp. and omit the olives and lemon.

Margaritas by the Jugful

Best made and served by the jugful, this delicious creation is one of the perfect outdoor cocktails. More ice means more dilution; crushed ice will give a "frozen margarita"—like a slush. Less ice means more pure intensity. Judge for yourself which style you prefer, but drunk alfresco it's usually easiest to shake the cocktail up with ice cubes and serve it simply. The salt rim is an essential. Serve with salted almonds (see page 20) or macadamia nuts.

Serves 8

Ingredients

1 1/2 cups gold or white tequila

1 cup Cointreau or Grand Marnier

1 1/2 cups freshly squeezed lime juice

fine sea salt, to decorate

8 lime wedges (optional)

2 cups ice cubes or crushed ice

To prepare/make Pour the tequila, liqueur, and lime juice into a large sealable jug, plastic bottle, or flask. Close and shake vigorously.

To present Put the salt into a shallow saucer. Rub a lime wedge around each glass rim. Invert each glass in the salt to crust it. Shake off the excess. Drop these lime wedges into the glasses. Stir or shake the margarita up with the measured volume of ice cubes until very cold. If using crushed ice, process in a blender. Pour the cocktail into the jug; pour out into prepared glasses.

Cubanaita Cocktail

A nutty, nonalcoholic, coffee-scented, refreshing cocktail or digestif.

Serves 4

Ingredients

4 tbsp. hazelnut syrup

4 tbsp. cinnamon syrup

1 cup decaffeinated coffee, chilled

8 ice cubes

chilled cola, to top up

8 lime slices or wedges

To make/present Combine the first 4 ingredients in a shaker or jug. Shake or stir well. Pour into 4 tall Collins glasses. Top each drink up with the cola. Add the lime slices and serve.

Index

Suppliers

Recommended stores where you can buy cooking equipment and other camping gear:

Eureka Camping Center
625 Conklin Dr.
Binghamton, NY 13903
888-638-3752
www.eurekacampingctr.com

North Face Inc.
2013 Farallon Dr.
San Leandro, CA 94577
www.thenorthface.com

REI
Sumner, WA 98352
800-426-4840
www.rei.com

For accessories such as plates, napkins, containers, rugs, and other decorative items:

Crate & Barrel
800-967-6696
www.crateandbarrel.com

eZiba.com
87 Marshall St.
Bldg. 1 at Mass MoCA
North Adams, MA 01247
www.eziba.com

IKEA
Plymouth Meeting Mall
498 W. Germantown Pike
Plymouth Meeting, PA 19462
800-434-4532
www.ikea.com

Pier 1 Imports
800-245-4595
www.pier1.com

Pottery Barn
800-922-9934
www.potterybarn.com

Restoration Hardware
15 Koch Rd. Ste. J
Corte Madera, CA 94925
877-747-4671
www.restorationhardware.com

Target
888-304-4000
www.target.com

Z Gallerie
1855 West 139th St.
Gardena, CA 90249
800-421-3372
www.zgallerie.com

Author's acknowledgments

Thanks to Bethany Heald, assistant food stylist, recipe tester and editorial assistant, and to Christine Boodle of Better Read Limited for her word-processing skills. The following food and wine suppliers and specialist shops have helped immeasurably in the evolution of this book:

Chalmers and Gray, Fishmongers,
of Notting Hill Gate, London W11

R. Garcia and Sons, Spanish Delicatessen,
of Portobello Road, London W11

Jeroboams Cheese and Wine,
of Holland Park Avenue, London W11

David Lidgate of C. Lidgate, Butchers and Charcutiers,
of Holland Park Avenue, London W11

Speck, Italian Delicatessen,
of Portland Road, Holland Park, London W11

Michanicou Brothers, Greengrocers, of Clarendon Road, London W11

Mr Christian's Delicatessen,
of Elgin Crescent, Notting Hill, London W11

Kingsland, The Edwardian Butchers,
of Portobello Road, London W11

Portobello Road stallholders and shopkeepers, of London W11, whose vivacity is a constant inspiration.